Museums and Memory

Museums and Memory

Edited by

Margaret Williamson Huber

Selected Papers from the Annual Meeting of the
Southern Anthropological Society, Staunton, Virginia
March, 2008

Robert Shanafelt, Series Editor

Newfound Press
THE UNIVERSITY OF TENNESSEE LIBRARIES, KNOXVILLE

Southern Anthropological Society
Founded 1966

Museums and Memory
© 2011 by Southern Anthropological Society: http://southernanthro.org/

Digital version at www.newfoundpress.utk.edu/pubs/museums
Print on demand available through University of Tennessee Press.

Newfound Press
University of Tennessee Libraries
1015 Volunteer Boulevard
Knoxville, TN 37996-1000
www.newfoundpress.utk.edu

ISBN-13: 978-0-9846445-2-0
ISBN-10: 0-9846445-2-0

Museums and memory / edited by Margaret Williamson Huber ; Robert Shanafelt, series editor.
Knoxville, Tenn : Newfound Press, University of Tennessee Libraries, c2011.
          1 online resource (vii, 239 p.) : ill.
          Includes bibliographical references.
1. Historical museums -- Southern States -- Congresses. 2. Southern States -- Antiquities -- Congresses. 3. Southern States -- Social life and customs -- Congresses. I. Huber, Margaret Williamson. II. Shanafelt, Robert, 1957-
III. Southern Anthropological Society. Meeting.
          GN36.U62 S685 2011

Book design by Jayne W. Rogers
Cover design by Stephanie Thompson

Contents

Figures

Tables

Introduction

Margaret Williamson Huber, University of Mary Washington

The papers that make up this volume were presented initially at the 2008 Annual Meeting of the Southern Anthropological Society in Staunton, Virginia, and all reflect its theme. A call to discuss "Memory and Museums" reflected the recent intense interest in the celebration of the 400th anniversary of the founding of Jamestown, Virginia; and Staunton itself, a living museum of nineteenth-century industrial Virginia enhanced by the American Shakespeare Center/ Blackfriars Playhouse and the Museum of Frontier Culture.[1] Although most of the papers focus on Southern memories, history, and museums, papers relating to other parts of the world are included as well. They also represent the different subdisciplines of anthropology— archaeology, cultural anthropology, linguistics, ethnohistory—as well as different modes of inquiry—oral history, artifact analysis, analysis of documents from various sources and periods.

In the diverse matters addressed in these papers, some common themes emerge. It is clear that a knowledge of the past is important to the people anthropology works with. This value is commonly expressed in terms of memory, whether a personal memory or the awareness of past figures and events. The importance of a knowledge of the past is great enough to suggest that responsible persons have an obligation to be aware of, to "remember," the past. These papers display also a distinction between a more official, centered "memory" (e.g., Jamestown) and an informal, local, peripheral one (e.g., the papers by Coggeshall and Probasco). A tension between the center and the periphery, and between the collective and the individual, is apparent in much writing about history, memory, and museums. The paper by Gable and Handler, which was presented as the keynote speech, addressed these issues, among many others.

The first two papers in this collection, by Jennifer Clinton and Tanya Peres and by Lynne Sullivan, Bobby Braly, Michaelyn Harle, and Shannon Koerner, focus on the archaeological and archival collections housed in museums—institutional memories, as it were. Although the papers deal with a different topic—Clinton and Peres test an hypothesis about hunting strategies among small-scale horticulturalists, Sullivan et al. discuss archives from the Depression-era excavations in Tennessee—both agree that the extensive but underused collections in museums are a rich resource for archaeologists, especially when rising costs severely limit the possibilities for new excavations or curating the artifacts once recovered.

The paper by Laura Galke and Bernard Means demonstrates the uses to which a modern institution can put archaeological and historical investigation. They describe how Washington and Lee University benefits from the results of recent and continuing archaeology and of ancillary archival research to confirm and project the sense of a long tradition of nourishing eager minds. As with the papers by Coggeshall and Probasco, we find that a venerable history adds both authority and authenticity to the institution. Washington and Lee, then, may be seen as a kind of museum, in that it presents to itself and to visitors ideas of what education should be and of what the university itself has been in the past.

Vincent Melomo offers a similar assessment of the Jamestown museums. Noting that the current exhibits go a long way toward recognizing the part Virginia Indians had in shaping the events of colonization and the success of Jamestown, he concludes that these museums, too, valorize modern middle-class Euro-America. He argues that since Jamestown is less about the past per se than a symbol of modern America, it should incorporate all modern ethnicities.

Making memories, as we know and as these papers demonstrate, is a primary function of museums. The paper by Avi Brisman provides a fresh perspective on this commonplace. He wonders what people remember, who view objects of art that have been stolen or have been subjected to vandalism such as graffiti, physical attack, erasure, even a kiss. Surely, he argues, anyone who now sees these pieces must include in their memories of the pieces the fact that they have been disfigured or stolen, which has to change how the pieces are appreciated. Objectively, if we regard the museum experience entirely in terms of memory, we cannot object to vandals or thieves since they but add to the collection of memories we have about particular works of art.

With Brisman's paper we move away from what museums want us to remember to consider what anyone remembers as an individual and how that affects one's perceptions of herself and her surroundings. The papers by John Coggeshall and Susan Probasco, respectively, address the latter questions. Instead of institutionally-sanctioned, official "memory," they give us the thoughts and memories of local people—in mountainous North Carolina, in a small Arkansas town—about the area they live in and how such memories reflect and influence their perceptions of those spaces, their affection for them, and their pride in living there. As with the paper by Galke and Means, we find that memories are bound up with places, and that a sense of things having endured adds luster and gravity to the things remembered.

Jennifer Nourse's paper gives us yet another angle on personal memory. She discusses photographs from her several field trips to

Indonesia over the past twenty years. The old pictures not only bring back memories, as one would expect; they also provoke reflection on her successes and failings as a neophyte, and then a more seasoned, anthropologist. The images span a period of time during which her personal life changed significantly, and so they recall earlier versions of Jennifer, even as they tell a story of an evolving ethnographic sophistication.

No collection of anthropological papers about memory would be complete without cross-cultural examples for comparison. Samantha Krause's paper about indigenous celebrations in San Miguel de Allende describes three annual festival processions that emphasize the idea of being Mexican. All focus on Mexico's indigenous past as well as its connection to Spain. These rituals are meant for the native people of the town, who organize and produce them, rather than to expatriate sensibilities or interests. Another important finding is that the Mexicans' ideas about authenticity differ from those of Americans. For the people of San Miguel, it is enough that a troupe of musicians looks something like Aztecs for them to be sufficient reminders of that part of Mexican history. Her paper reminds us that ideas about memory, history, and "truth" are not shared universally.

The final paper in this collection, by Heidi Altman and Tom Belt, makes this point even more forcefully. Using primarily linguistic material from the Cherokee, they show that Cherokee ideas of memory, even after centuries of contact with European culture, differ considerably from Euro-American ones, not least in the fact that memory can have a real effect on the well-being of the physical body.

The first paper in this collection, that of Eric Gable, of the University of Mary Washington, and Richard Handler, of the University of Virginia, makes challenging points regarding the anthropology of memory and of museums. Chief among these is an examination of the use of the term "memory." Strictly speaking, they point out, the phrase "collective memory" is an oxymoron, since neither a society nor a culture has the capacity for thought or memory. They argue that even if it is proper to talk of a collective memory, neither museums nor histories can give us memories of what they celebrate. Only those who have experienced the events can truly be said to remember them, and even then what is remembered is one's own immediate involvement. Rather, museums and monuments inform each of us of the past in some particular way and insist that we add it to our consciousness—that we remember it. In that regard, they suggest persuasively that "memory" as it is presently studied is little different from culture.

The first question Gable and Handler ask, though, is why memory should now be so "trendy" in anthropology and allied disciplines. The answer to that question can tell us much about modern American culture. As they observe, studying memory is also to study what is forgotten, and modernity—also known as progress—is accompanied by forgetting as new, "improved" things replace what has been. Nostalgia and the fear that the past will entirely disappear motivate, however paradoxically, much of modern culture. But it is demonstrable that these ideas have their own history in our discipline, albeit in a different form. In the remainder of this essay I review our involvement with these themes and suggest additional reasons for our concern, as anthropologists and as a nation, with the remembrance of things past.

II

Cultural anthropology in the United States began with memory. This took two forms: the intensive recording of indigenous custom and, as a part of that, the collection of indigenous memories of their own past.

The nineteenth-century certainty that the native cultures—indeed, the peoples—of the Americas were doomed to extinction, victims of modernity, moved anthropology to set as a primary goal the rescue and recording of as much of those cultures as possible while there was still time. Natives themselves shared this pessimistic view. The collaboration between Eli Parker and Lewis Henry Morgan came about because Parker, convinced of the impending obliteration of his people's culture, seized the opportunity to have Morgan record it in order to prevent its complete disappearance. The same bleak anticipation shows in Benedict's reported comments from her Digger informant Ramon: "'In the beginning…God gave to every people a cup, a cup of clay, and from this cup they drank their life.…They all dipped in the water…but their cups were different. Our cup is broken now. It has passed away'" (Benedict 1934, 21-22). Convinced that time was running out, and likewise of the virtue of preserving in the memory customs and concepts that might never again appear in the world, early American anthropologists and their informants together created a great treasury of information about indigenous cultures.

But even then, anthropologists were certain that these same cultures had been distressingly changed by the European presence. Here, memory played a different role in the conservation of North American native custom. Because they were less interested in what they saw as a diminished, inauthentic version of the "true" native culture than in its "pristine" antecedents, our early ethnographers asked their oldest informants to remember what they could about life during their youth, and to mine their memories for what their parents and grandparents might have said about *their* younger days. By means of memory, supplemented by archaeology and linguistics, they hoped to discover what life was really like before Europeans arrived. Only later did we come to realize that these memories, like the cultures themselves, might be influenced by changed circumstances, and so might be more about the present than about the past. This is a critical point in the study of memory, and of history, and I return to it below.

If the main purpose of early American ethnography was the preservation of the minutiae of the past, another was to figure out the broad sweep of prehistory in this continent. A careful amassing of authentic, pre-contact details from all over would allow the determination of culture areas; to identify the points of origin of cultural inventions such as the Sun Dance, and to find the centers of cultural climax. What later were called "the people without history" would be given a history, one that stretched back in time as far as archaeology would let us go. True, that history could not tell us what the people who created and developed it thought about what they were doing, but it might give us some idea of the impersonal forces that affected independent invention and cultural diffusion, resistance or accommodation to cultural change. If we knew the past, we could understand the present, specifically the present state of North American Indian cultures.

The themes of memory, authenticity, and history, then, have been with us from the beginning. We may add to these concerns that of the individual. Just as anthropology was emerging as its own discipline, so too was psychology, a subject that deeply interested American anthropologists. Their wish to merge the two approaches to studying human beings evolved into the personality-and-culture school of anthropology and then into the current concern with identity.

The study of memory, at once intensely personal and ultimately social, should give us a means of identifying and understanding the interplay between the collective and the personal, the social and the psychological. It is crucial in the concurrently emerging study of identity as well. We are concerned with memory because we want to know the basis for identity. The philosophical postulate that a person knows who she is by what she remembers (e.g., Heath 1974, 24; cf Sturken 1997, 1) has been metaphorically applied to social groups, who likewise refer to their "collective memories" as a basis for distinguishing themselves from other groups. Halbwachs's (1980 [1950]) argument that memory is social lies at the center of this way of thinking. According to him, we remember things, we remember them as we do, and we rely on our memories in particular ways all because the process of socialization teaches us to do so. Sociality gives coherence, and therefore meaning, to our memories, otherwise a jumble of sensory impressions; meaning is essential to remembering. Perhaps it was unwise of Halbwachs to call this a collective memory, since it can be taken to imply that somehow the congeries of people in a society have linked mental functions, like the alien children in John Wyndham's *The Midwich Cuckoos*. But he may be guilty only of elision. A human being is a person, not just a biological entity, because she belongs to a society; the way she thinks, including the nature and function of her memory, is due to her being a part of that society; therefore, in a sense, it is a collective memory even though no two people's memories are exactly the same, as Halbwachs himself points out. Or, as Dumont (1970, 39) says more generally, "…[a person is not] a particular incarnation of abstract humanity, but…a more or less autonomous point of emergence of a particular collective humanity, of a *society*." Autonomy implies choice; collectivity, the bases for choice. Likewise, Halbwachs's collective memory, from a certain point of view, allows both idiosyncratic recollection and an explanation for the general similarities of memories "shared" by members of a society.

Tracking the history of thinking about the past, memory, and the individual (or, preferably, the person) and society in American anthropology is beyond the scope of this essay and is, anyway, unnecessary. The matter is important here only because of its influence on the modern anthropological interest in memory. We think of the focus on memory, and on history, as a comparatively recent phenomenon, one which appeared either in tandem with an equally recent American obsession with commemoration (Sturken 1997, 11), or as a result of it. Either way, though, what we think of as a new focus of study turns out to be but the most recent manifestation of perennial American anthropological questions.

Putting the recent resurgence of interest in these matters into a context to help us understand that it is an old problem justifies this summary history of American anthropology. The allied topics of individual and collective memory, history, authenticity, and the relation of the individual and society turn out to be perennial issues for us. Because it constrains our questions and the way we interpret the answers we get, it reproduces itself in the practice of our discipline.

This may be the answer to the question why is there the overwhelming interest in these topics in anthropology today. That is, there is interest because these are not new concerns; rather, they are old issues in American anthropology, as old as the discipline, and we are still trying to arrive at a satisfactory understanding of them. But there is more to the matter than simply a structure of the *longue durée*. Long, after all, does not mean eternal.

History alone can explain neither persistence nor present meaning. Trying to do so amounts to a tautology. No one denies that knowing the history of a people or a custom is interesting and may be informative. What we need to ask is, of what are we being informed? The fact that a thing has a past—which is always true and is therefore not informative—cannot explain why it has persisted or why the people in the present find it worthwhile to do. One has only to look at the numerous vanished cultural forms to realize that persistence is not automatic. On the contrary, we might suppose, given the current rate of cultural impoverishment in the world, that disappearance is more likely than persistence. What we want to understand are the *reasons* for the continuities, alterations, or extinctions of cultural ideas and forms.

There is another reason to delve further into the importance of memory in modern anthropology. To say that these issues have salience because of the nature of American anthropology is too one-sided a view of the situation. American anthropology did not develop an interest in memory and the rest in a vacuum. Almost every people we know—the BaMbuti of the Ituri Forest may be an exception (Turnbull 1961, 1965)—has a history (sometimes called myth) and insists on its importance, meaning that at least some of the people have to remember it. They share with modern Americans not just a value for history but also for the authority of the person who knows that history, and all that that implies about becoming someone of note and resource and maintaining that status once achieved. As ethnography has found repeatedly, authority depends on a superb memory and skill in imparting one's knowledge to others.

And we have found that knowing history is important because history everywhere is perceived to have explanatory power. At its simplest, this conviction takes the form of that notorious answer to the anthropologist's "why": "We've always done it that way." But more specific historical explanations—including Malinowski's charter myths—justify locations, economies, rituals, names, marriages, murders, affinities, antipathies, conversions, rejections—in short, everything people do. That culture and history are one and the same appears to be a logical conclusion. Thus the celebration of history—including the insistence that historical events be part of our "collective memory"—seems not only reasonable but necessary in order for a people to maintain their sense of themselves and their values. The current anthropological interest in memory, which is to say history, is justified both logically and because of the interests of the people we want to understand.

Some problems with this argument still remain, however. What does it mean to say that history and culture are the same thing? There is no generally satisfactory answer to this, but the question must be asked if only in a cautionary way. If the two are the same thing, then the proposition should be reversible. Our sense, though, is that they are complementary rather than mutually replaceable. History is the past, and culture is its latest manifestation, the most recent chamber on the shell of the nautilus. Culture is contingent, not just on history, but on what we remember of our history; but the reverse is not true. Only in fantasy is it possible to go back and change history; and even there the author often arranges things so that the time-traveler is not really changing anything at all but rather doing something necessary for her or his present to be as it should.

But as many recent students of memory, including some of the authors in this collection, have observed, there is in fact something like a reciprocating relationship between culture and history. On the one hand, we may say that we know, as a necessary thing, that whatever modern culture or cultural form we study has a past, a history; and that its present form is contingent on that history. But we also realize that the history that our informants tell us is "about" the present day, their current concerns and convictions and categorical relations; and we recognize that our own history, too, is about ourselves in the present. Vincent Melomo's paper in this collection argues that Jamestown, as a symbol of the United States, should find some way to celebrate all the constituent sub-populations of the modern United States even though there were not, strictly speaking, Latinos or South Asians in North America in 1607. His point is that since we use the past as a way to represent to ourselves our own present, we should do a thorough job of it, and not leave bits of the present out. Such an argument is itself a reflection of the present, with its attentive concern over the people history forgot because they "had no history." The paper by Lynne Sullivan et al. likewise expresses a modern sensibility in its critique of the photographic documentation of WPA and CCC archaeological workers during the Depression. The photographers concentrated on the white males and virtually ignored the considerable number of African Americans—women and men— and white women who contributed their labor and knowledge to these projects. The fact that today we would not be so blind, or not in that way, makes us aware of the blindness of our predecessors. The story we tell of the past is conditioned by our own concerns about how stories should be told. We conclude that all people do the same thing with their histories because the great weight of ethnographic evidence persuades us that way.

But, as we can see from these papers, American attitudes to history—and, thus, to memory—present a paradox. Even as we acknowledge that the interests of historians at any given time reflect their contemporary concerns about what is important and how to understand society, we also insist that the history we Americans tell be authentic. If we contemplate the material remains of the past, they must either be real remains or else re-create the original faithfully and be clearly labeled "reconstruction." If we focus on events, they must be real events, and we must know how they really happened. "Real" in this case means "verifiable," and the only way to prove that an event happened is with material evidence: documents and photographs, artifacts, and soil stains; and by an exhaustive recovery of such proof. It also means that the only acceptable point of view is that one has none; or, rather, it means that as anthropologists we want to bring to the study of history the same objectivity that we try to bring to ethnography. Anachronism is temporal ethnocentrism.

Our history must be authentic in terms of appearance and detail, and it must represent correctly the world view of the people whose culture we study.

Can these two understandings of history—that it is about the present, that it must only represent the past—co-exist? The logical answer is no. And in many cases they obviously do not. History whose purpose is to explain the present ignores anything that seems irrelevant to the production of that present. For example, the Renaissance is presented as the beginning of the modern world, especially modern science. Such histories treat Renaissance excursions into alchemy—when they discuss it at all—as regrettable, because conceived in error, but necessary because they led to the invention of chemistry. As Dame Frances Yates has shown repeatedly, however, treating Renaissance thought in this way leaves us ignorant of its true nature (Yates 1964, 1969, 1972, 1979, 1996). There was at that time no separate category of "science" as it is understood today. The point was to understand God's creation; to that end, anything could provide insight, both in itself and in how it was related to other things. Their way of classifying things was not that of the present: they saw connections among phenomena (the planets, stars, colors, precious stones, periods of time, body parts and substances) that today we regard as so disparate as to call superstition any attempt to relate them. To dismiss this way of thinking, though, leaves the Renaissance essentially a closed book; and that means, in turn, that we cannot explain what they thought they were doing.

And that was to be themselves, not to be the midwives for modern life (Trouillot 1995; Sahlins 2000, 9-10 et passim). So to regard the events of the past as *merely* the prologue to the present is a futile undertaking. It leaves us in the dark about what we want to explain because it refuses to accept as valid any contemporary customs or ways of thinking that do not lead happily to the present day. In short, history would appear to be an impossible discipline, since if it is really about the present it cannot be about the past, and since we cannot escape the constraints of our modern culture we can never write about the past in any other terms.

The burden of this paradox is evident in many of the papers in this collection. As they write about memory, museums, and the representation of history, the contributors understand the attention to detail and to the participation and concerns of all the actors in the event countering the inherent ethnocentrism of much history. Such scrupulous reporting, they argue, should, and does, come ever closer to revealing the truth, which is to say, the whole objective truth.

In the insistence on authenticity and detail, however, modern Western history betrays modern Western concerns. As Krause's paper, for instance, shows, for modern Mexicans "authenticity" does not depend on factually correct detail. Likewise the paper by Altman and Belt reminds us that ideas about memory and history vary considerably from culture to culture. There are many ethnographic reports that counter the idea that there can be only one history, too. Lest we forget, we raise monuments everywhere, and we take extraordinary pains to make finely detailed representations. We commemorate the horrific in our history in order, as many have concluded, to make comprehensible the apparently random and meaningless (Linenthal 2001a, 16, 228; 2001b, 7; Sturken 1997, 2); we also celebrate the quotidian for something like the same reason (Sturken 1997, 1; Ernst 2000, 28). The past must be remembered in order to give meaning to the present—to show, perhaps, that it is better, or that it could be—but also because we have come to see forgetting the past as a moral failing analogous to massacre, even genocide.

To put the matter thus is not to explain it but to pose in different terms the original question of why have we become so driven to remember our past(s). The restatement may nevertheless provide some insight into the problem. A concern with the welfare of oppressed minorities and marginal peoples characterizes much of modern life. These groups are hardly novel in human history; but we may fairly say that feeling obliged to take them into account and, if possible, reverse their fortunes is something new, or uncommon anyway. The same concern extends to the non-human world, too, where species and habitats appear to be threatened or eradicated with increasing frequency. So we are called upon to remember the victims of colonial and capitalist indifference and to join in concerted attempts to halt atrocities in Darfur, wage-slaves in Mexico, political suppression in Tibet, racist covenants in the United States.

Implicit in these appeals is the notion—touched on earlier—that what is central is of less moral value than the peripheral. Before dismissing this suggestion as an overgeneralization, consider the widespread American distrust of government (resulting, in one famous case, in the bombing of a Federal office building), including the conviction that while a candidate for office may be fairly honest she or he will inevitably become corrupt once elected; the dismissal of "dead white males" from many curricula in favor of "native," minority, and women's voices, and the corollary refusal to acknowledge that a colonial voice is as valid as a native one; the increased attention to the marginal, voiceless peoples of history. Examples could be multiplied, but these should be enough to justify the assertion that virtue is nowadays found mainly in the margins.

That the modern American conscience about the world's unfortunate people finds expression also in concerns about how to think about and remember the past is hardly surprising. To forget—to ignore—the contributions of the humble, whether Native Americans or Africans or European peasantry—to modern American life and culture has become as unprincipled as refusing to intervene in Rwanda or Zimbabwe. Even less acceptable is indifference—forgetting—about victims of violence in America—those killed in 9/11 or in Oklahoma City or even in automobile accidents. As forgetting becomes tantamount to indifference, memory becomes evidence of engagement.

III

There is another important aspect to the current stress on remembering the past, distinct from, but allied to, concerns about restoring the displaced to the pages of history and to our memories. This is Gable and Handler's suggestion that it is a reaction to modernity, which blatantly and aggressively replaces the old with the new in the name of progress, leaving people feeling rudderless in the face of change. I suggest that the will to progress is not modernity's only threat. The progress, if we should call it that, has certainly happened. Since the end of the Second World War our daily activities have altered almost out of recognition, from the electronic explosion and the resulting ubiquity of computers and the Internet to a cuisine in which hummus, tacos, and pad thai are ordinary foods. The material conditions of life are, for many people, much better than they were seventy years ago. Society has made some progress as well. Gender and racial barriers have been eroded, if not yet done away with, and the general expectations about minority groups radically changed as well.

These are, no doubt, changes for which to be thankful; certainly they are goals for which many have struggled and some have died. Why then should there be so profound a mistrust, indeed a dislike, of modern life as seems to be prevalent in America today? This may, of course, be a pointless question. Trouillot observes that "history is messy for the people who must live in it" (1995, 110); the corollary would appear to be that the past will always be more appealing because we know how it comes out. But this is not necessarily so. Ambiguous situations, uncertainty about the future, and recognition of change occur in every culture, but the obsessive recording and preserving of the past do not; nor is the past always perceived as preferable to the present.[2] It might be argued that what matters is the degree of change and, therefore, of ambiguity and uncertainty. But that argument founders on the fact that right now we are not, in fact, progressing very much. Change there is, but it is what Goldenweiser (1936, 102-3) called involution and Kroeber (1948, 329) called the exhaustion of the pattern. All the possibilities of the old pattern have been explored, so that now it constrains rather than provokes innovation; and no new pattern has emerged to replace it. Our only option is to rework what we already know. Whether borrowing from previous style in the design of a new automobile or a building or zealously guarding the evidence of the past, we affirm that we do not, in fact, have any new ideas. Distressingly, the reworking of the old ideas rarely yields anything as pleasing as the originals. Thus we have come to expect that the next new thing must certainly be worse than what it replaces. The materials will be shoddier, the workmanship cruder, the appearance more appalling. In such an atmosphere, conservation becomes a moral obligation if we are to have anything of value in our environment.

It is hard not to see this distrust in terms of capitalism. The speed with which jerry-built developments, malls, convention centers, and hotels rise amongst us suggests inevitably the greed of the developers, who appear to have no respect for the past, for the environment, or for the sensibilities of the public. Their only interest is in the maximum quick return on their investments. Popular culture frequently casts these people as the bad guys. Conservation, on the contrary, is perceived as a selfless undertaking, since the investment of time and money is intended for the general well-being of the public, not the swelling of a private bank account. Such philanthropy is itself considered an antique virtue, consonant with its object of preserving the things of the past as well as its ethos.

An important aspect of that ethos is the perception that in the past America experienced more social solidarity than now. If alienation is a consequence of capitalism, then we may suppose that the country today is in fact less a commonwealth than at any time in the past, and this perception has some validity. Tocqueville, for instance, argued that the democratic principle fostered alienation; but he also admired the contemporary American determination to counter that by forming associations—sporting clubs, literary societies, charitable organizations, lodges. But the facts, in this case, are less important than the general certitude that in the past we had communities, but nowadays we have the individual.

Alienation, which is to say capitalism, may be to blame for much of this pessimism. But there is another contributing factor as well. Fussell argues persuasively that modern memory is heavily charged with irony because of the disastrous course of the First World War: a string of ill-judged policies, broken promises, failed assaults, betrayed troops, wasted resources. The *normal* situation was "all fucked up." Everyone came to expect that nothing would go right and that those in charge could not be trusted. Fussell does not deny that irony formed a part of literature long before the Great War. What he does say is that it was never pervasive. On the contrary, the tone of earlier literature was generally buoyant; trust and optimism were not considered naive. The unprecedented calamities of the War, however, made it impossible for people any longer to sustain that attitude; and the cynicism that replaced it has continued, even increased, to the present day, fuelled by such events as the Vietnam war, Watergate, the Iran-Contra affair, and the first and second Iraqi wars. In such an atmosphere, the past assumes the mantle of Truth as well as of Order. This conviction itself contributes to the current insistence that history not only be true but be the whole truth. If, ironically, that means revealing the failings of past leaders, nevertheless, the knowledge can be a source of hope for the present: that modern historians are honest and that a good many of the wrongs they report have been made right.

In its devotion to a cult of the past, American culture bears a startling resemblance to that of the Renaissance, which was also a period of pessimism and of glorification of the past. Deeply disturbed by the schisms in the Church, and especially by the violence attending them, many sought to re-create the Roman empire, which they perceived to be a period of wide-ranging and long-lasting peace. To this end they focused intensively on the correct use of the Latin language on the premise that if it were again in constant use, the culture that produced it would in some sense be resurrected. Americans have not adopted the speech of their forebears, but we do seem to be persuaded at some level that a return to the built and the natural environments of the past will bring about a welcome restoration of our former society.

Kroeber observed a century ago that any important cultural form had many motivations, implying that the more important the form, the more complex its origins. The great importance we place on remembering—whether one's own ancestors or the nation's history—springs from a number of sources, some of which I have tried to identify in this essay. That all these influences have converged in this way leads one to think that this is a cultural concern that will not soon disappear, neither from popular culture nor from anthropological enquiry.

NOTES

1. Carrie Douglass was in charge of local arrangements. She proposed the theme and suggested many of the papers included in this volume.

2. In a fascinating study of Victorian domestic life, for example, Judith Flanders demonstrates that the Victorian reaction to social and cultural change was an intensive definition and segregation of social and cultural categories: public and private, male and female, master or mistress and servant, work and play, inside and outside, and degrees of cleanliness (Flanders 2003).

WORKS CITED

Dumont, Louis. 1970. *Homo Hierarchicus: The Caste System and its Implications*. London: Paladin Books. Originally published as *Homo Hierarchicus: Le système des castes et ses implications* (Paris: Editions Gallimard, 1966).

Ernst, Wolfgang. 2000. "Archi(ve)textures of Museology." In *Museums and Memory*, edited by Susan A. Crane, 17-34. Stanford: Stanford University Press.

Flanders, Judith. 2003. *Inside the Victorian Home: A Portrait of Domestic Life in Victorian England*. New York: W. W. Norton.

Goldenweiser, Alexander A. 1936. "Loose Ends of Theory on the Individual, Pattern, and Involution in Primitive Society." In *Essays in Anthropology Presented to A. L. Kroeber*, edited by Robert H. Lowie, 99-104. Berkeley: University of California Press.

Halbwachs, Maurice. 1980 [1950]. *The Collective Memory*. Translated from the French by Francis J. Ditter, Jr. and Vida Yazdi Ditter. With an Introduction by Mary Douglas. New York: Harper and Row.

Heath, Peter. 1974. *The Philosopher's Alice*. New York: St Martin's Press.

Kroeber, A. L. 1948. *Anthropology*. New York: Harcourt, Brace.

Linenthal, Edward T. 2001a. *The Unfinished Bombing: Oklahoma City in American Memory*. Oxford: Oxford University Press.

Linenthal, Edward T. 2001b. *Preserving Memory: The Struggle to Create America's Holocaust Museum*. New York: Columbia University Press.

Sahlins, Marshall. 2000. *Culture in Practice: Selected Essays*. n.p.: Zone Books.

Sturken, Marita. 1997. *Tangled Memories: the Vietnam War, the AIDS Epidemic, and the Politics of Remembering*. Berkeley: University of California Press.

Trouillot, Michel-Rolph. 1995. *Silencing the Past*. Boston: Beacon Press.

Turnbull, Colin M. 1961. *The Forest People*. New York: Simon and Schuster.

Turnbull, Colin M. 1965. *Wayward Servants The Two Worlds of the African Pygmies*. New York: Natural History Press.

Yates, Frances A. 1964. *Giordano Bruno and the Hermetic Tradition*. Chicago: University of Chicago Press.

———. 1969. *Theatre of the World*. Chicago: University of Chicago Press.

———. 1972. *The Rosicrucian Enlightenment*. Boulder, CO: Shambhala Publications.

———. 1979. *The Occult Philosophy in the Elizabethan Age*. New York: Routledge and Kegan Paul.

———.1996. *The Art of Memory*. Chicago: University of Chicago Press.

Forget Culture, Remember Memory?

Eric Gable, University of Mary Washington
Richard Handler, University of Virginia

In this paper[1] we want to ask what anthropology can contribute to that increasingly ubiquitous topic, the study of social memory. To do this we will first sketch why we think memory has become such a trendy term. Next we will outline what we see as some similarities and differences in the anthropological concept of culture and the concept of memory as it is routinely deployed in the social sciences and in cultural studies broadly conceived. To anticipate our conclusions, we will argue that for anthropology to contribute to the study of social memory, anthropologists must be as relentlessly critical of the idea of memory as anthropologists have been critical of culture, their own favorite term. Indeed, as we hope to show, "culture" and "memory" are parallel concepts, sometimes useful, sometimes not. Sometimes the terms reveal and illuminate, sometimes the terms obscure and get in the way of our capacity to understand and interpret what people are doing and thinking in this place in this moment in time.

Both culture and memory obscure or get in the way when they become inappropriately anthropomorphized. Cultures do not think or feel. Societies do not remember. And the individual, as conceptualized in modern ideology, is not necessarily the socially defined agent that "bears"—that is, possesses—memory or culture as if they were things. Worst of all, both "culture" and "memory" get in the way of our ability to interpret when these terms allow us to import into one society a world view that is native to another, mistaking the local for the universal. Memory and culture are native concepts after all. As such they are especially relevant when we wish to understand the native point of view of contemporary cultural-studies discourses—discourses that currently have a global reach. But for the study of native points of view that do not participate in those discourses, these terms can, as often as not, be a dangerous distraction.

TRENDY MEMORY

So, why is memory such a hot topic today? Clearly part of the answer involves our current, we might say personal, preoccupation with forgetting. This preoccupation is a constant topic in the news and popular press. Figuring out how to stop or stave off forgetting is becoming a huge business. Hundreds of researchers in psychology departments all over the U.S. and Europe are busy trying to discover the chemistry of how we remember and forget. Forgetting is associated with Alzheimer's syndrome and aging: everything from "where did I put my keys" to "who am I—or you?" In the vernacular, I am my memories. If I forget too much, I lose myself. So, in societies like ours, with its demographic bulges and troughs, the media bombards us with stories and images of the pathos of forgetting, not to mention a plethora of remedies—Sudoku, crossword puzzles, a daily dose of exercise or gingko biloba. The ubiquity of our preoccupation with forgetting in a society such as ours limns and adds luster to the scholarly fascination with the topic.

But let us not forget that memory in the scholarly literature outside of psychology is a shorthand for a social rather than a personal phenomenon. Memory in this literature is social memory. It is associated with everything from monuments to the crude propaganda totalitarian regimes make; from public to popular imaginings, aided by the media, for example, of the holocaust or Vietnam. Memory in this sense is rarely personal, even as individual people may literally remember—as if it happened to them—what they saw on TV or read in a book, or heard from a friend or family member. "Memory" in this sense in the scholarly literature is a shorthand term for a host of images, words, and ideas collectivities share and communicate which are all more or less associated with the past. For making "memory" such a trendy umbrella term to refer to a grab bag of social practices associated with imagining the past we can thank—or blame—cultural historians.[2]

Just as we are personally anxious about forgetting, so too does it seem that the scholarly fascination with memory among cultural historians and other scholars in the social sciences and in cultural studies broadly conceived is driven by a certain anxiety—an anxiety such scholars associate generically with modernity, but also more specifically with those great modern transformations we call revolutions or revolutionary upheavals, from the French and American Revolutions and the Industrial Revolution to the rise and fall of the totalitarian regimes in Germany and Russia. Such transformations are said to have led to pronounced shifts in the historical imaginations of the affected peoples, and perhaps to the end of history itself.

No wonder, then, that modernity has long been associated with loss. Modernity is primarily a story of progress, but progress always entails loss. To go forward you must forget, yet you regret what you no longer recall so you collect souvenirs, mementos. Modernity is always nostalgic. Nostalgia, for the most part, remains a shadow of the idea of progress. But in times of crisis, so the scholarly wisdom goes, nostalgia becomes a sort of refuge. Thus nostalgia is a common theme in the discourses of the new emerging nationalisms of the post-modern era. And this is not surprising given that a common assumption of nationalists is that nations, like individuals, require a past to have an identity.

The politics of nostalgia in new nations, or in newly transformed old nations, makes memory an obvious topic for cultural historians, but it hardly explains why they have chosen the term "memory" to encapsulate this complex set of discursive practices. We might also look at recent disciplinary shifts to get a handle on why so many historians like the term "memory." Here it is important to stress a venerable distinction historians make between history and memory. Historically at least (forgive the pun) historians have tended to dismiss memory as inferior to the material traces of the past, especially to documents—to text. From the perspective of historiography, memory used to be by and large what savages or illiterate peasants have. It was what idiot savants excel in or what racial inferiors rely on and do so well. Horses or dogs or monkeys might have more of it than "we"; that is, literate or educated or cultured people, did. Don't forget, Thomas Jefferson's systematic assault on the mentality of people of African descent entailed that he granted them a superior memory because their minds were inferior. Indeed, for Jefferson, it was the extraordinary memories of blacks that made them dangerous. Better, he argued, to ship them back to Africa than to free them here in America, where they would endlessly recall and seek bloody retribution for the scars of their enslavement. Because they remembered too well they could never be citizens of the same nation as their erstwhile masters who, while they defiled themselves in the institution of slavery, were at least more intelligent, more balanced in their capacity for reason and thus would get over the corrupting influences of their collective past (Jefferson 2002).

Thus in Jefferson's day memory was inferior mental capacity—a reflex as it were. As with Jefferson, so too with historians. Animals remember and human inferiors remember; historians and moderns in general do not because they neither need to nor want to. They can rely on the superiority of the text and the document to do their remembering for them, and in any case, memory fades and warps with the passage of time. The document, by contrast, if properly stored and protected, lasts forever and speaks forever of that past moment in which it was produced.

Historians read such a record. And "memory" is a term that allows them to put distance between the work they do—making objective histories in the form of scholarly treatises or popular books, making histories in the form of museum exhibits, documentaries, or lectures—and what the common folk, but also increasingly the state, that sinister abstraction, also does. Once "memory" is a term distinct from history, cultural historians can also allow themselves to write histories about the work of memory either as a popular impulse or a state project. Note that historians tend to fall into two camps when they write their histories of memory. Either they expose memory's elisions and erasures or they celebrate its capacity to expose, reveal, critique. In the first instance memory is routinely conflated with the official activities of the state or the state's other analogs—the corporation, the ruling class, the powers that be. The common trope is that of substitution. The state manufactures memory for the people who, as a result of their exposure to the state's narrative, forget what they themselves experienced or heard from their elders or their compatriots. In this scheme the state makes uniform memories in order to order. They build monuments, host celebrations (the anniversary of this or that battle, or war, the beginning of a nation, the birthday of a president), edit and teach school books, and produce films all to make a past that serves their purposes into a memory that each citizen or subject has. In the second instance, memory is imagined as a popular and persistent eruption. Memory, despite all those monuments and publicly endorsed stories, or better yet, because of their sheer bombastic monumentality, their kitschiness, cannot be squelched. Popular memory rises up, like a fart or like bones from a shallow grave, to contest official accounts.

Like bones from a shallow grave because the idea of popular memory reeks of a certain kind of past. The past of totalitarian regimes, of state-initiated violence, of gas chambers, mass executions, death squads, of the disappeared—of a politics, in short, of repression and of resistance, to repression, however feeble.

Like a fart because memory in this view is often a kind of low subversion—a weapon of the weak, to borrow James Scott's apt phrase (Scott 1985). Thus, for example, in East German cities before the wall came down buildings cratered or scarred by shrapnel were often marked with a plaque commemorating "Evidence of Allied Bombing," while in a theatre playing a film celebrating the Red Army's conquest of Berlin, when a tank was shown destroying a building with a single well placed shot, someone in the audience could use the darkness to remark out loud, "Evidence of Allied Bombing," and others could laugh at the quick joke at the state's expense.

So, for cultural historians the work of memory is obviously political, engaged. It is therefore important to be on the right side of the struggle, usually the subaltern side. This does not mean, however, that historians restrict themselves to romancing memory as a kind of revolutionary return of the repressed. The best of them are well aware that memories, even the popular kind, are not to be taken at face value. Indeed, like those anthropologists such as Michael Taussig who celebrate the surreal and fantastical in popular imaginings, so too do cultural historians know that subaltern memories might be equally fictional, like magical realism, while remaining allegorically true.

THE EVASION OF CULTURE

Now that we have suggested why memory is so trendy, linking memory as an idea to recent disciplinary shifts in cultural history, we would like to ask: what is the relationship between culture and memory, as anthropological concepts? To approach an answer to that question, consider another: what is the place of anthropology among the social and cultural sciences?

One answer to the second question, surely not wrong, is that anthropology *in theory* studies global human diversity, which has meant that *in practice* anthropology has focused on all those peoples that the other social sciences ignored, especially those peoples once called primitive and now called, perhaps, "peripheral" or "marginalized" or merely "non-Western"—there is no good term. Indeed, the fact that all such terms designate those societies we imagine most unlike us points to an important truth about the social sciences. With the exception of anthropology, they all conflate humankind with one, and only one, of its varieties, the modern Western world. As Louis Dumont (1977; 1986) has argued, from the seventeenth century onward, the gradual formation of the social sciences—political science, economics, sociology, psychology—corresponded to, and indeed mapped, modernity's emerging understanding of the social world as partitioned among a number of discrete domains (the state, the economy, society, psyche, and so on). The discipline of history is founded on a similar move, for, as Daniel Segal (2000) has shown, the modern concept of history presupposes a notion of "prehistory"—the time before writing—that excludes much of humanity from consideration by historians. By definition, history is, as Segal (2000, 772) ironically remarks, "post-prehistory."

To the analytically fragmented vision that the social and cultural sciences both map and project, anthropology opposes its own holistic understanding of humankind. Yet, anthropologists have two quite distinct ways to conceptualize holism. The more common of the two, as represented in the American four-field approach, has been formulated from *within* the modern worldview and, more important, is content to reproduce its analytic categories. In this view, which Clifford Geertz (1973) once called stratigraphic, anthropology entails a pragmatic bundling of separate disciplines that, taken together, can analyze humankind in all its dimensions and, adding up the results, as it were, arrive at a holistic vision of humanity. These disciplines are, of course, "the sacred bundle" of biological anthropology, archaeology, linguistic anthropology, and sociocultural anthropology. If we add to these such latter-day sub-disciplines as political, economic, ecological, psychological (and so on) anthropologies, we can find within anthropology all the other social sciences and, indeed, several humanities and science disciplines as well.

But according to Geertz, Dumont, and others, there is a very different kind of anthropological holism, one that is not stratigraphic, one that insists on cultures or societies as potentially incommensurable wholes. We stress the word "potential" here because you do not have to imagine such wholes as hermetically sealed in order to grasp, nonetheless, the idea that there are no one-to-one correspondences between the categories of one such cultural world and those of another. From the perspective of this kind of holism, there is no reason to believe that the modern categories enshrined in our university curriculum are the right ones to use if one's concern is to understand other, non-Western, social worlds. "Economics," "politics," "art," and "religion" are not to be found everywhere.

Indeed, from the perspective of this second kind of anthropological holism, we must call into question, or suspend our use of, not only our disciplinary categories, but some basic cross-disciplinary concepts that all the social and cultural sciences presume. These include the distinction between individual and group (whether we refer to the group dimension as society, polity, or culture) and the habit of conceptualizing entities at both the individual and group level as internally homogeneous, neatly bounded, and possessed of agency. A final set of presupposition we should suspend concerns the question of social order. Although various theoretical strands in Western thought privilege "change," "conflict," or "miscommunication," the social and cultural sciences in general start from the notion that social order is the fundamental fact, and, further, that order is to be understood as sharing, whether the stuff that is shared is imagined as physical substance (blood), cultural symbols (including memories), or economic and political interests.

While "culture" has been the dominant concept of American anthropology since Boas, the term has repeatedly come into conflict with, and been temporarily rejected in favor of, concepts like "economic base," "social structure," and more recently "identity," "practice," and finally, yes, "memory." We want to argue that in all of these theoretical disputes of the last 70 years or so, the implicit battle has been between the two kinds of anthropological holism. From the analytical perspective of the first kind of holism, which tries to sum the causal force of various "layers" of social reality (the economic, psychological, social, and so on), the individual-group dichotomy remains a governing presupposition. That is to say, "the individual" remains a privileged analytic unit, and the problem comes to be seen as how to weigh the causal significance of the "forces" that act upon the individual as they emanate from the various social domains. In the end, this approach always reduces the social to the sum of individually experienced actions and decisions. Even the forces of culture and society are conceptualized, by social scientists, in terms of how they affect individuals, and, through individuals, the groups to which they belong.

From the perspective of the second variety of anthropological holism, however, there is no reason to suppose that the "individual versus group" dichotomy is universally relevant. Certainly we should not imagine these terms as universally and equally salient in all cultures. As Dumont (1977, 8) puts it, individual persons are empirically present in all societies, but the individual, as a morally autonomous agent imagined in contradistinction to society (itself imaged as a collection of individuals and a collective individual with its own agency) is a peculiarly modern phenomenon.

When we forget that the individual-versus-society approach is grounded in our own native understandings, and when we turn those understandings and concepts into analytic categories, we find ourselves confronted with an unsolvable problem: which is more important, for explanatory purposes, the society or the individual? The dilemma is impossible because, as anthropologists, we know that individuals are shaped by their social surroundings, and that, in some sense, they cannot exist apart from it. Similarly, we know that societies or cultures are "composed of" individuals, and that all social actions and forces must in some way emanate from individual human beings. As Ruth Benedict once rather plaintively asked, "where else could any [culture] trait come from except from the behavior of a man or a woman or a child?" (1934, 253).

Despite the fact that the individual-society dichotomy presents an impossible dilemma, fashions in the social and cultural sciences tend to swing back and forth between both its poles. When, for example, structuralism of one sort or another becomes too obviously unreal—when, that is, it becomes increasingly unconvincing to lodge explanatory power in impossibly remote patterns or structures available only at the end of an exquisite and difficult analysis—then theoretical fashion begins to swing back the other way. Not pattern but the individual, not structure but action or practice, not culture but identity, not ideas but material realities and the on-the-ground actions of real human beings, and so on.

And, of course, not history but memory. We remarked earlier that we have cultural historians to thank or to blame for making memory such a hot topic. As anthropologists, we should thank them because they opened up a field of study—of monuments, of museums, of ceremonies and mythologies—in short, of rituals and representations that have always been the bread and butter of anthropology. No wonder that we have increasingly taken to this terrain as we, as a discipline, have shifted our field from out-of-the-way places and the savage slot back home, as it were, to the nation and the state.

But we can also blame them for making "memory" a term of art because this term—which, after all, is psychological and individualistic, and which at best is a metaphor drawn from the level of the individual to talk about social and cultural phenomena—leads to the reproduction of the individual-society dichotomy. As such, it confines the social and cultural sciences within the well-worn grooves of modern Western individualism. And it replaces the mysteries of cultural, symbolic phenomenon—those processes whereby human individuals are never merely individuals as Westerners imagine them to be, just as societies or cultures are not collective objects—with that fatiguing analytic process of tacking between the psychological and the social.

MEMORY AND THOUGHT

If "memory" belongs to a set of terms that are made to represent the individual pole of the individual-society dichotomy, it nonetheless differs from such terms as "practice," "action," and even "the individual." "Memory" refers not to material or on-the-ground realities, as those other terms do, but to mental phenomena. We attribute mental phenomena easily enough to the individual, and thus memory anthropomorphizes, as we said at the outset. Yet, of course, the mystery of culture is located (conceptually, as it were) at the point where brain becomes mind; that is, where individuals *become* individuals (and culturally defined ones, at that) *only* through cultural processes that are in the end not individualistic. Is it useful, we now ask, to think about memory as a particular kind of thought, and if so, how does memory differ from culture itself?

To begin, let us note that "memory" is a peculiar, if predictable, term to use when one is writing about what people collectively or as individuals imagine they know about the past. It is peculiar even if one begins by stressing that in a strict sense every thought a person has is a memory. Thoughts are after the fact and are never the facts themselves, but representations, constructs. Yet, in the strict sense every memory is also a thought. "Memory," "thought," and "imagination" are words we routinely deploy to speak about the same mental process.

For historians, "memory" is the term of choice because it privileges mental activity as an historical endeavor. *Homo historicus* remembers, has a memory. In anthropology thought has often been reified in a parallel fashion. People think, of course, just as they remember, but we tend also to say that societies have a memory or that they have a "culture," which, scratch the surface of that term, assumes that they have thought. Culture, in the platonic sense, is Thought (the capitalization is always implied), thought embodied, to be sure, in objects, words, rituals, and so forth—all those models of and for that Geertz made famous—but nevertheless thought: personality-writ-large, mentalité, and all that. Cultures are like people in that they have systems of thought. So, given the obvious dangers, what benefit is there to calling memory "thought," or thought "memory"? In both we have inappropriate anthropomorphization. People think or remember, but societies do not have memory or thought. Clearly they do not remember or think.

In a semantic sense, thought privileges the present, memory the past. But memory also privileges, inadvertently, a directly experienced, if warped or transformed, past. Yet most of the past, as a congeries of representations that interest cultural historians and anthropologists, is not this kind of past at all. Rather it is nothing more or less than an indigenous practice of communicating about what is in the past. It is a practice that usually blurs the boundary in time between moments experienced by the living and the dead. It is a practice that routinely blurs the boundary between what is experienced and heard or read. For the two of us—and we would suggest that we share this view with many in anthropology—this indigenous practice of communicating about the past can be called "history," and "history" can be roughly defined as a story of the past made out of words, images, and objects, often in combination. History in this sense is what historians make. But it is also what anthropologists have sometimes called "myth" when it is a story some savage tells us about distant events that savage claims happened at or near the beginning of time. When scholars such as cultural historians write about collective memory, or social memory, or vernacular memory or official memory, or sites of memory, and then generally in a sentence or two deploy, as a shorthand for these, the word "memory," we would substitute for that word "memory" the word "history." We do this for two reasons. One, history avoids the easy and inevitable anthropomorphizations. History is not as immediately or obviously a personal experience. It is an account, a narrative that you tell about something you objectify as a past. Second, history purposively blurs and confounds the distinction cultural historians see, and want to maintain, between history as a written product, more or less objective, and memory as a popular conception, often oral, occasionally accurate, usually distorted, that is shaped by passion and prejudice, that reflects the desires and fears of the teller, that has to be scrutinized and evaluated in the light of other evidence.

Any anthropologist knows that what people claim to remember is, to put it crudely, a cultural fiction. But by the same token so are the histories historians write. Note that even those historians most engaged in the study of social memory are often not willing to challenge the hegemony of history over memory. They may well know something we anthropologists might insist upon: that as conveyers of cultural information, documents are no more "reliable" or "objective" than any other kind of cultural object. Beyond that, documents can be downright duplicitous. Documents can be erased or forged; and thus they can infect memory, replacing partial truths with absolute lies. Historians may well know this, but they ignore it as they go about their business.

It begins to seem, then, that the distinction between "memory" and "history" speaks rather to our own notions of the individual in relationship to society, and "amateur" (or individual) knowledge versus institutionally (or socially) produced expertise, than to a useful epistemological distinction between types of thought. Indeed, we would go further and say that the use of the term "memory" in the social and cultural sciences is yet another example of the canonization of our own "domaining" of knowledge and our expectation that terms drawn from those domains can serve universally, in any and all cultural settings.

What, then, of the relationship between the terms "memory" and "culture"? From the first approach to culture that we outlined above, the stratigraphic approach, "memory" is another term that allows us to compare the causal significance of individual forces in relation to those that are social. But from the second approach to culture, which seeks for a holism that does not rely on the Western stratigraphic model of what society is, there does not seem to be much utility in distinguishing the terms "memory" and "culture" for purposes of a cultural analysis of human thought. After all, what in culture does not implicate some sort of symbolic reference to what has gone before the present moment (the only moment in which thought can "occur")? And what in memory is not "always already" culturally structured? To put this another way, given an adequate theory of culture as symbolic process, and accepting the term "memory" as one that Western natives use to talk about themselves, is there any reason to use memory as an analytic construct at all?

THE PAST FROM THE NATIVE'S POINT OF VIEW

The answer, to anticipate our conclusion, is only when such a term is an indigenous one. When they talk about memory, then we must listen to them. But when we analyze what they say about "memory," we inevitably embed that term in a larger cultural context. When natives in our society, at least, are talking about the past as a representation, "memory" is always a term that shadows "history," or more prosaically "the past." To show you what we mean, it might help to leave the terrain of abstraction to look at things on the ground. After all, anthropology really only comes into its own when it is conveyed as ethnography.

So let us briefly revisit our experience of studying at Colonial Williamsburg and Monticello—places cultural historians would clearly recognize as a "sites of memory," but places we prefer to call "museums," "public history" sites, even "shrines," because these terms hew more closely to the words our native interlocutors use when they describe these places to us. When we did research we constantly found ourselves asking: "How is the past imagined and discussed at these sites—from 'the native's point of view'?" And we did so because our natives too were preoccupied with that question. Let's start with Williamsburg, and to simplify we will look at the question from the perspectives of two kinds of natives—first, those who managed it and used it to communicate to the public about the past; second, those whose job it was to ensure that visitors kept returning to the site as satisfied consumers of what the place had to offer.

Among those who worked at Williamsburg as educators (and that includes frontline guides or "historic interpreters," their managers and higher-level administrators (including historians), we rarely heard the word "memory" used except as a pejorative term, something the visiting public brought with them that got in the way of learning about the real past. Visitors, it was said, sometimes misremembered the place—talking about tours that never happened or recalling objects sold in gift shops that never existed. Or more often they remembered the way the place used to look and wanted it to stay that way. But scholarship—that is, historical knowledge—was always advancing, so the landscape, the architecture, the decor and even what was told about these had to change. Confronted with these changes—paint left to peel or go dingy on the exteriors of buildings; for example, or paint applied in gaudy and clashing colors to erstwhile austere interiors—made visitors angry and above all mistrustful. They assumed the worst about Williamsburg—that it was trying to do things on the cheap, or that it had substituted plebian tastes for patrician ones.

Memory in this sense got in the way of the work of communicating about the past. The presence of memories in the minds of visitors required that visitors not only had to be taught about the past itself but endlessly reminded of Williamsburg's good intentions. Indeed perhaps the salient feature of a place like Williamsburg was how much pedagogical work involved what we came to see as impression management. Managing the impression visitors had about the site

entailed stressing the disinterested work of historiography. New facts
would be found and historians followed those facts where they led.
Inaccuracies, especially anachronisms, were in turn blamed on the
visitors themselves. Trees on the Duke of Glougchester Street? Well,
these remained because the public assumed that old tall oaks and
the past were one and the same, and besides they liked the shade.
Gardens full of boxwoods, or doorways decorated with wreaths?
Well, these remained because that's what visitors also wanted and
expected, and remembered.

If educators at Colonial Williamsburg often blamed visitors for
clinging to an inappropriate memory of the past or for remembering
what clearly never occurred, those who were charged with selling the
site to the public used "memory" in a very different, even contradictory way. In advertisements and brochures visitors were encouraged to
come to Colonial Williamsburg to make memories or have memorable experiences. Such talk of memory is hardly surprising. It has long
been recognized that in modern consumerist societies, as Antze and
Lambek stress in their excellent summary of memory studies (1996),
"memory" is conflated with "experience" and both are imagined as
things to be possessed. In the case of Williamsburg, like so many
similar sites, what was sold as memorable conflated both the peda-
gogically useful and the personally gratifying. Parents, so the modal
trope had it, could take children to Colonial Williamsburg and their
brush with the past would make them better at school, more capable
of retaining the arcana of their school-based history lessons because
they had had a memorable experience chatting with an historical
interpreter in a costume while eating colonial-era food in a tavern or
seeing sheep grazing in a field while the smell of wood smoke filled
the air. But this pleasurable, pedagogical memory enhancement was
also advertised as producing memory in a more personal way: being
with family and having fun as a family were equated with producing

the kinds of memorable experiences that would become the mortar of family bonds. As a rule Williamsburg did not disappoint in producing such memorable experiences. Indeed, that is why so many visitors returned, say, as adults with children of their own, eager to show them the militia marching down the street, eager to have them taste Brunswick stew or eat a smoked turkey leg held in their fist, so as to revisit the magic of their childhood memories.

Needless to say, we found it fascinating that the production of such memorable experiences was as often as not at odds with the larger pedagogical objectives of the site. They created the very visitor who would complain if things changed—if the current Williamsburg was not like the Williamsburg they remembered and cherished. The paradox was that personal memories were at once manufactured by the site and trivialized. Thus it is that the consumer slouches into the sites of public history in modern societies.

At Monticello, in contrast to Colonial Williamsburg, memory has in recent years been politicized because of its conflation with race and racial difference. We probably do not have to remind any of you of the convoluted controversy of Thomas Jefferson's alleged affair with Sally Hemings, a slave. But it is worth recalling that before the DNA evidence was accepted with alacrity by the Thomas Jefferson Foundation as likely proof that Jefferson and Hemings had produced offspring, the controversy pitted what both sides in the controversy called African American "memories," passed on via "oral tradition," against what the Foundation saw as the judicious weighing of evidence by historians whose written products could be taken as an antidote to rumor and myth.

African Americans have a word for this kind of history. They call it "his story" because it is the story "the Man," the master, the powers that be; write or tell about the past in order to cover up or hide or otherwise lie in self-serving ways about what really happened. And they like to recount personal experiences of encounters with "his story" at the moment of its manufacture, thereby stressing its contrivance. Thus it was that many African Americans could speak from what they considered to be their personal memory of visiting Monticello and seeing the infamous stairway that led from Jefferson's alcove bed to a secret chamber where Hemings waited quietly for safety of the night. Barbara Chase-Riboud, author of a novel (i.e., fiction) that so irked Monticello's staff because it made so many visitors skeptical about the Foundation's claims to honesty (Chase-Riboud 1979), asserted in an interview in 1994 that the stairway was removed shortly after the bestselling novel came under ruthless attack by various historians. "They ripped it out on July 4th 1979, leaving a gaping hole... What kind of rage must they have experienced to do that?" To this charge, Monticello's director Daniel Jordon conceded in the obligatory reportorial counterpoint that the stairway was indeed removed, but that it led only to a storage closet, not a hiding place, while also insisting that the stairway "was probably installed in the Victorian era."

Needless to say, Jordan's response might sound to skeptics a lot like "his story" all over again. But what fascinated us just as much was his deployment of the judicious "probably" because it typifies what we came to see as an uncomfortable fact about public history at places like Monticello and Williamsburg: the troubling absence of text when text is most needed. Monticello and Williamsburg are sometimes referred to as if they were texts. Clearly they are complexly produced and reproduced congeries of objects whose very objectivity makes them hard to ignore, hard not to experience as facts. But despite their objectivity, they are as factual as a memory or, for that matter, the books historians write. Over time, decisions are made about what to hang on this wall or plant in that garden bed, what to pull out or to rearrange. At every step in this process, documents are consulted, but so too are guesses made, inferences. These inferences sometimes are documented—a memo in an archive—and sometimes they are not. Thus it is that at Monticello, for example, if you visit the house today you encounter a map of Africa hanging prominently in the entry hall along with Indian artifacts and mastodon bones, not to mention the Great Clock and the concave mirror. This room was in Jefferson's day a museum of sorts—a cabinet of curiosities. The map of Africa, though, never hung in that room. Why it hangs there today is a mystery we have tried to solve. At present our best guess is that it reflects a curatorial decision, one of several, to make Africa, or rather African Americans, a more prominent part of the kind of community of memory Monticello has been endeavoring to create since the mid-nineties. But we can only guess because, while the moment of its hanging is recorded, the origins of that decision have been forgotten and leave no trace in any archive. Thus it is that "his story" becomes history, or at least a fact you may or may not notice when you tour Monticello today.

CONCLUSION: FORGET MEMORY?

We began by asking why "memory" is so trendy and why, because it is so trendy, anthropologists might do well to keep their distance from this term. At the same time, we have suggested that we pay attention to what natives say and do.

If native conceptions of what we call the past are not structured in terms of Western theories of history and memory, then it does little good to analyze those conceptions in terms of ours. Trying to apply an oxymoron like "social memory" to worlds that do not already presuppose the Western dichotomy of the individual versus society makes it too easy to rewrite their psychology, and their epistemology, in terms of ours.

In the study of Western societies, however, where forgetting has become a paradigm of loss in the face of progress, anthropologists will have to pay attention to the native discourse of memory. The trick here is to remember to include social scientists and historians among the natives. Thus we found, at the history sites we have explored, a studied endeavor to forget or overlook the similar processes that occur in the production of history and the production of personal memories. Not to be conspiratorial, but there is clearly a purpose, if inadvertent, in such forgetting. At both Monticello and Williamsburg, the purveyors of public history can continue to imagine that what they do is based on written texts, on real facts, on disinterest rather than passion or prejudice. Others, inferiors—people they must patronize—have memories. They, by contrast, possess history. Yet from the analytic perspective we have outlined here, history and memory are one and the same. They are discourses about the past constructed from the perspective of the present. They are "cultural" in the anthropological sense of the term, and they are patterned in the way culture is patterned, holistically.

NOTES

1. Presented as the keynote address to the Southern Anthropological Society, Saturday, March 15, 2008, University of Mary Washington, Staunton, Virginia.

2. There is an enormous literature on social memory, which we do not review in this paper. Especially useful to us has been the volume edited by Paul Antze and Michael Lambek (1996) as well as several reflective essays by historians (Confino 1997, Crane 1997, and Kansteiner 2002).

WORKS CITED

Antze, Paul and Michael Lambek, eds. 1996. *Tense Past: Cultural Essays on Trauma and Memory.* New York: Routledge.

Benedict, Ruth. 1934. *Patterns of Culture.* Boston: Houghton Mifflin.

Chase-Riboud, Barbara. 1979. *Sally Hemings: A Novel.* New York: Viking.

Confino, Alon. 1997. "Collective Memory and Cultural History: Problems of Method." *American Historical Review* 102:1386-1403.

Crane, Susan M. "Writing the Individual Back into Collective Memory." *American Historical Review* 102:1372-85.

Dumont, Louis. 1977. *From Mandeville to Marx: The Genesis and Triumph of Economic Ideology.* Chicago: University of Chicago Press.

————. 1986. *Essays on Individualism: Modern Ideology in Anthropological Perspective.* Chicago: University of Chicago Press.

Geertz, Clifford. 1973. *The Interpretation of Cultures.* New York: Basic Books.

Jefferson, Thomas. 2002. *Notes on the State of Virginia.* Boston: Bedford/St. Martin.

Kansteiner, Wulf. 2002. "Finding Meaning in Memory: A Methodological Critique of Collective Memory." *History and Theory* 41:179-97.

Scott, James C. *Weapons of the Weak: Everyday Forms of Peasant Resistance.* New Haven: Yale University Press.

Segal, Daniel A. 2000. "'Western Civ' and the Staging of History in American Higher Education." *American Historical Review* 105:770-805.

Evaluating Mississippian Period Hunting Strategies at the Rutherford-Kizer Site

Jennifer Clinton and Tanya M. Peres,
Middle Tennessee State University

EXISTING COLLECTIONS ARE THE KEY TO ANSWERING NEW QUESTIONS

The use of existing collections in answering new questions is timely and important. Museum curators and archivists across the country are faced with tight curation budgets and limited storage space, so that it is not always justifiable to excavate sites to collect specimens (Stankowski 1998). Using existing collections for modern research is important on several levels. Stankowski (1998) notes that artifacts "spend 99% of their time in storage," and "the key to finding funding for curation is to actively use the collections." The Arizona Governor's Archaeology Advisory Commission (2006) suggests "encouraging or even requiring more use of existing collections rather than new fieldwork" as a solution to the curation crisis. It is difficult to persuade policymakers, private citizens, and corporations to fund curation of collections that are never seen by the general public nor used for research by scientists.

Museums, universities, and state and federal repositories around the country house archaeological collections from many sites that have been subsequently destroyed and even forgotten. These collections offer archaeologists opportunities for research and learning, without the added expense of fieldwork. Recent studies of archaeological collections from Middle Tennessee and Kentucky by faculty and students at Middle Tennessee State University highlight the kinds of information we can retrieve from existing archaeological collections. Some of these sites were excavated in the mid-twentieth century when the focus was on culture chronology, but the materials from those digs provided answers to current questions in archaeology, ranging from prehistoric subsistence strategies to gender to inter- and intra-group violence. This study is a prime example of the effectiveness of using existing collections and published data as media for undergraduate student and faculty research collaborations.

INTERPRETING HUNTING STRATEGIES IN MIDDLE TENNESSEE CIRCA AD 1000-1400

The goal of archaeology is to interpret past human behaviors based on observations of material culture. Zooarchaeologists apply this principle to ancient food remains in order to determine patterns of human hunting, foraging, fishing, and agricultural practices. The goal of our study is to identify how anthropogenic changes of prehistoric landscapes, coupled with scheduling conflicts for resource procurement, is realized in the faunal assemblage of one late prehistoric site in Middle Tennessee.

It is widely accepted that people living during the Mississippian Period (AD 1000-1400) in the Southeastern United States practiced a system of agriculture that was centered on growing domesticated imported crops such as maize—and, later, beans and squash—as well as native cultigens such as sumpweed and sunflower. To harvest surplus yields of crops successfully to feed the food-producing and non-food-producing segments of society, fields larger than house gardens were necessary. This would require landscape management and modification, generally clearing of forested areas that were cycled through periods of cropping and fallowing. As VanDerwarker

(2006, 148-149) points out, "an increasing focus on farming to meet basic subsistence needs likely involved the reorganization of the larger subsistence system," and "scheduling other subsistence activities like hunting and fishing would have become more difficult."

GARDEN-HUNTING AS RISK MANAGEMENT: A SURVEY OF MODELS AND CASES

Several models of garden-hunting outline the archaeological corre-lates of certain actions related to this subsistence strategy. Linares (1976) proposed the original "garden-hunting" model. Linares' model was designed for sites in the American tropics, specifically Panama, but it is applicable beyond that environment. This model suggests that humans were selective in the animals they targeted, specifically larger mammals. Human populations focused nearly exclusively on a few big game animals while they were abundant. The shift in focus to these large mammals, especially in areas where the dietary tradi-tion included aquatic fauna, would lead to a shift in dietary focus (i.e., to the near exclusion of the aquatic taxa) (Linares 1976). More recently, however, ethnographic studies have shown that large game populations, if hunted exclusively in and around agricultural fields and gardens, were easily overexploited (see VanDerwarker 2006, 149 for a discussion of this). To identify Linares' selective garden-hunting strategy we can turn to the site-specific zooarchaeological record. According to this model, the faunal remains will consist of animal taxa that travel in small numbers over small ranges, that tend to be passive, and that are adapted to living in edge environments. These animals are easy to catch in traps and favor cultivated crops for their diets. The game populations can withstand heavy predation and recover quickly. The faunal assemblage will include predomi-nantly larger terrestrial animals versus small mammals and aquatic fauna (Linares 1976).

Neusius (1996), building on Linares' work, proposed a revised model of garden-hunting designed for the Dolores Anasazi in the American Southwest. This model suggests that humans were more opportunistic and non-selective and would hunt any animal that was available. Neusius' model relies on the assumption that cultivated fields contain a high diversity of plants and would therefore have a corresponding high diversity of animals. Archaeologically, the faunal assemblage will contain high species diversity in comparison with natural spaces, and the represented species will be the most able to tolerate cultivation changes (Neusius 1996, 280). This model is also supported by the fact that cultivation places further constraints on time. Local human groups would have had little time for hunting, so they merely gathered what game they could, where they could (Neusius 1996).

A third case study of the garden-hunting model is VanDerwarker's interpretation of garden-hunting in relationship to the Olmec of Mesoamerica (VanDerwarker 2006). VanDerwarker's (2006, 151) current model is similar to the other models; she argues, however, that this sort of diversification represents risk management. The "entire premise of the garden-hunting strategy is the economy of resources," and that local human groups chose a "selective or opportunistic approach depending on availability" (VanDerwarker 2006, 151). There is an organic continuum between selective or opportunistic within VanDerwarker's model as well. Archaeologically, VanDerwarker's model is much the same as the Linares and Neusius models. She suggests that farmers could be more selective in the animals hunted when crop harvests were good. Conversely, when crops failed, farmers may have used a "take what you can get" approach to hunting animals in and around their fields (VanDerwarker 2006, 151). This more opportunistic strategy would result in zooarchaeological assemblages with high species diversity (VanDerwarker 2006).

VanDerwarker uses the zooarchaeological data from two Olmec sites, La Joya and Bezuapan, to test the garden-hunting model. At La Joya, people selectively hunted specific animals, as shown by the high number of large terrestrial "disturbance" mammals in the assemblage from the Early through Late Formative periods. VanDerwarker interprets this as an indication that "farming had become a more dependable and less risky venture" (2006, 164); however, during the Terminal Formative period at La Joya, the people expanded their hunting territory by exploiting animals from aquatic and primary forest environments. VanDerwarker (2006, 165) suggests that the people living at La Joya during the Terminal Formative were dealing with some degree of dietary stress that was likely related to "local environmental catastrophe (volcanic eruptions and ashfall)."

The patterns at Bezuapan faunal assemblage are slightly different. It appears that hunting of large terrestrial mammals increased early on, leading to overexploitation of these prey species. Thus, people had to diversify and hunt a wider range of smaller taxa to supplement their diets. VanDerwarker suggests this increase in the range of animals being exploited reflects management of subsistence-related risk as the residents of Bezuapan invested "more time and labor into agriculture" (2006, 177-178).

Modern ethnographic research supports several aspects of the garden-hunting model as well. Naughton-Treves and colleagues (2003, 1112) conducted research in the Peruvian Amazon, which showed that "shortly after maize was planted, wildlife visits to the disturbed areas peaked and was statistically higher than the amount of wildlife that visited fallow fields or forests." This research also showed that areas that were too heavily cultivated did not attract the number of animals necessary to balance crop losses with protein gains (Naughton-Treves et al 2001, 1107). Therefore, this subsistence strategy is best employed in areas of low human population density.

Ethnographic evidence shows that both selective and non-selective strategies are employed (Neusius 1996, 275). The choice depends on the reliability of the agricultural yields (VanDerwarker 2006, 150). In areas were agricultural yields are predictable and high, agriculturalists are more likely to hunt with increasing selectiveness. The choice between selective and non-selective may also depend on the gendered division of labor (VanDerwarker 2006, 150). Cultivation is an intensive strategy for food production and requires large inputs of time and energy. As humans cleared more land in the past, they provided the opportunity for an increase in the diversity of edible vegetation, which led to an increase in animals attracted to these cleared areas with easily edible cultivated crops (VanDerwarker 2006, 148). By adopting a garden-hunting scheme, populations would be able to hunt with no special preparation, as was required for hunting parties, since it took place in cultivated fields and home gardens. It was far less time-consuming because it happened while performing other cultivation requirements. Garden hunting was also low risk because it often involved traps and snares (VanDerwarker 2006, 149-150). It would reduce competition for a farmer's resources by killing the larger pests that could destroy the crops; and this hunting strategy provided reasonably easy access to protein, so much so, in fact, that garden hunting might have served as a substitute for animal domestication in the New World.

The animals that gardens attract have a special set of characteristics. Certain animals (e.g., white-tailed deer and turkey) are attracted to disturbed environments such as home gardens or forest edges because of the concentration of crops and weedy plants, which attract insects and browsing taxa (Neusius 1996; VanDerwarker 2006). Linares (1976, 347) refers to these animals as commensals, while VanDerwarker (2006, 149) and others refer to them as crop pests. They usually travel in small packs, and they are not overly aggressive, and therefore need smaller home territories. For example, white-tailed deer need a home range size of about 49-120 hectares, while a black bear's home range size can be up to 26,000 hectares. The local animal populations can recover quickly from overexploitation and other population pressures. The best example of this characteristic comes from Linares's research at Cerro Brujo in Panama, where the inhabitants relied far less on white-lipped peccary than on the collared peccary because the white-lipped peccary pack sizes are large and dangerous to hunters without guns (Linares 1976, 347).

If farming groups practiced a selective strategy for balancing protein needs with agricultural activities, we would expect to find a relatively higher proportion of large versus small terrestrial mammals and relatively few aquatic animals. If an opportunistic strategy were employed, we can expect to find a high species diversity (many different types of animals) represented by a relatively high number of smaller prey animals. We tested the garden-hunting model using published data from the Rutherford-Kizer Site, located in Sumner County, Tennessee (Figure 2.1).

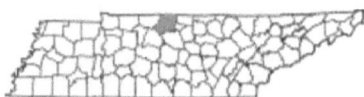

Figure 2.1. Sumner County, Tennessee. Location of Rutherford-Kizer Site. Map Source: http://en.wikipedia.org/wiki/Sumner_County,_Tennessee

THE RUTHERFORD-KIZER SITE

The Rutherford-Kizer Site (40SU15) is a late prehistoric mound center located in the Nashville Basin along Drake Creek, a tributary of the Cumberland River. Previously published radiocarbon dates for the site range from AD 1280 to 1485, placing Rutherford-Kizer in the middle Mississippian Period (Moore and Smith 2001, 73). Professional and avocational archaeologists have excavated at the site for over 100 years (Moore and Smith 2001, 1). From 1993 to 1995, the Tennessee Division of Archaeology (TNDOA) excavated the site as a direct result of modern urban growth.

The Rutherford-Kizer Site is situated at the higher elevations of the outer rim of the Cumberland Basin on a primary tributary of the Cumberland River (Moore and Smith 2001, 11). The terrain around the site is characterized by Maury-Braxton-Harpeth soils, which are "deep, well-drained, clayey and silty" (Moore and Smith 2001, 12). Some of the best upland farming occurs in this area of Tennessee today. The site occurs in what is known as the Western Mesophytic Forest Region, characterized by "oak, hickory, tulip tree, beech, and chestnut" (Moore and Smith 2001, 12). Most of Middle Tennessee lies within the Carolinian Biotic Province, which is distinguished by large game such as white-tailed deer, elk, and black bear; smaller game such as bobcat, otter, and cottontail rabbit; birds such as owl, turkey, and duck; as well as a variety of snakes, frogs, turtles, fish, and mollusks (Moore and Smith 2001, 12).

The Rutherford-Kizer Faunal Assemblage

Emanuel Breitburg analyzed the faunal assemblage recovered during the Tennessee DOA excavations, and the data were published as part of the site monograph (Breitburg and Moore 2001). We use Breitburg and Moore's published data (summarized below) as the basis for our model testing.

The faunal assemblage from Rutherford-Kizer consisted of 8,563 specimens, represented by 30 species, 9 genera, 5 families (See Table 2.1). Mammals comprised the majority of the assemblage at 71% (n= 6,709). Birds comprised 16.7% (n= 1,427), reptiles 9% (n= 774), amphibians less than 1% (n= 7), and fish 4.4% (n= 380). Just over 20% of the assemblage was identifiable to at least family (n=1,726). Of the identified fauna, white-tailed deer (*Odocoileus virginianus*) comprised the majority (n=787, nearly 46%). Eastern box turtle (*Terrapene carolina*) comprised 15% (n=262), and wild turkey (*Meleagris gallopavo*) 8% (n=141). The subsistence trend at Rutherford-Kizer shows a reliance on white-tailed deer, wild turkey, and box turtle, which is not unexpected, based on previous zooarchaeological research by Peres (see Peres 2006; Peres et al. 2005).

TAXON	COMMON NAME
Vertebrata	**Vertebrates**
Mammalia	**Mammals**
Mammalia, Large	large mammals
Mammalia, Small	small mammals
Didelphis virginiana	Oppossum
Scalopus aquaticus	common mole
Canis familiaris	domestic dog
Canis lupus	gray wolf
Canis sp.	fox size
Urocyon cinereoargenteus	gray fox
Mephitis mephitis	striped skunk
Procyon lotor	Raccoon
Ursus americanus	black bear
Cervidae	deer, elk, wapiti
Cervus canadensis	elk, wapiti
Odocoileus virginianus	white-tailed deer
Rodentia[1]	rodents

TAXON	COMMON NAME
Castor canadensis	Beaver
Marmota monax	Woodchuck
Ondatra zibethicus	Muskrat
Oryzomys palustris	marsh rice rat
Sciurus spp.	Squirrels
Sciurus carolinensis	eastern gray squirrel
Sciurus niger	eastern fox squirrel
Tamias striatus	Chipmunk
Sylivilagus floridanus	eastern cottontail rabbit
Aves	**Birds**
Branta canadensis	Canada goose
Colinus virginianus	Bobwhite
Meleagris gallopavo	wild turkey
Strix varia	barred owl
Grus canadensis	sandhill crane
Corvus brachyrhynchos	American crow
Ectopistes migratorius	passenger pigeon
Anas spp.	Ducks
Passerine	perching birds
Reptilia	**Reptiles**
Testudines	Turtles
Terrapene carolina	box turtle
Chelydra serpentina	snapping turtle
Chrysemys/Graptemys spp.	sliders and cooters
Trionyx ferox	softshell turtle
Serpentes	Snakes
Crotalidae	non-poisonous snakes
Viperidae	poisonous snakes
Amphibia	**Amphibians**
Rana / Bufo sp.	frogs and toads

TAXON	COMMON NAME
Osteichthyes	**bony fish**
Amia calva	Bowfin
Catostomidae	Suckers
Moxostoma sp.	Redhorse
Ictalurus spp.	Catfish
Ictaulurus punctatus	channel catfish
Aplodinotus grunniens	Drumfish
Cyprinidae	Minnows

Table 2.1. Identified Taxa, Rutherford-Kizer Site (40SU15).

Species Richness and Equitability

The first component of the analysis is the diversity of species in the Rutherford-Kizer assemblage. We addressed assemblage equitability using the Shannon-Weaver function. According to this function, assemblages with an even distribution of abundance between taxa have a higher diversity than samples with the same number of taxa, but with disproportionately high abundance of a few taxa. Samples that have a high number of taxonomic categories and a similar degree of equitability have greater diversity values (Reitz and Wing 1999, 105). We used estimates for the Minimum Number of Individuals (MNI) for identifiable taxa, with values computed by Breitburg. The Shannon-Weaver function indicates that the Rutherford-Kizer faunal assemblage, while rich (s = 41 taxa), is not equitable (V' = 0.033). This means that the faunal assemblage is dominated by one or a few taxa, specifically white-tailed deer (MNI = 24 or 21% of the total MNI) (Table 2.2). Overall, the richness and equitability values suggest that the residents of Rutherford-Kizer, while exploiting animals that preferred disturbed and forest-edge environments, were doing so selectively.

COMMON NAME	MNI	%MNI
Oppossum	2	1.74
Common mole	2	1.74
Domestic dog	2	1.74
Gray wolf	1	0.87
Gray fox	1	0.87
Striped skunk	2	1.74
Raccoon	1	0.87
Black bear	2	1.74
Elk wapiti	2	1.74
White-tailed deer	24	20.87
Beaver	1	0.87
Woodchuck	1	0.87
Muskrat	1	0.87
Marsh rice rat	7	6.09
Eastern gray squirrel	5	4.35
Eastern fox squirrel	7	6.09
Chipmunk	1	0.87
Eastern cottontail rabbit	2	1.74
Canada goose	1	0.87
Bobwhite	2	1.74
Wild turkey	9	7.83
American crow	1	0.87
Barred owl	1	0.87
Sandhill crane	1	0.87
Passenger pigeon	1	0.87
Duck	1	0.87
Perching birds	1	0.87
Box turtle	10	8.70
Snapping turtle	1	0.87
Sliders and cooters	1	0.87
Softshell turtle	2	1.74

COMMON NAME	MNI	%MNI
Non-poisonous snakes	1	0.87
Poisonous snakes	1	0.87
Frogs and toads	1	0.87
Bowfin	1	0.87
Suckers	2	1.74
Redhorse	1	0.87
Catfish	1	0.87
Channel catfish	5	4.35
Drumfish	5	4.35
Minnows	1	0.87
Total	115	100.00

Table 2.2. Minimum Number of Individual Estimates for Identified Taxa Rutherford-Kizer Site (40SU15).

Terrestrial vs. Aquatic Animals

Linares' (1976) garden-hunting model indicates that fully agricultural groups would be more dependent on terrestrial animals than on aquatic animals. While Linares makes this argument from a diachronic stance, the level of data analysis that exists for Rutherford-Kizer does not allow us to follow suit. Instead, we look at the relative MNI quantities of terrestrial vs. aquatic animals to test this portion of the garden-hunting model.

There are 24 taxa that live primarily in terrestrial environments and 13 from primarily aquatic habitats. Those taxa that were identified to class or genus, but include species that live in terrestrial or aquatic environments, were excluded from this analysis (i.e., *Rana/ Bufo* sp.). When percentage MNI was calculated based on this habitat division, terrestrial animals comprise about 79% of the assemblage, while aquatic animals are just under 21%. These data suggest that the residents of Rutherford-Kizer relied most heavily on terrestrial animals, especially those that are attracted to agricultural fields and house gardens.

"Disturbance Taxa"

Anthropogenic land clearing, whether for agricultural fields or the construction of buildings, disturbs habitats. These newly cleared habitats can sustain a greater diversity and density of animals than the same areas before they were cleared (VanDerwarker 2006, 159). VanDerwarker suggests (2006, 159) that the presence of disturbed habitat animals in a zooarchaeological assemblage can be the function of two types of human choices/activities: (1) human modification of the local environment; and (2) explicit targeting of those animals that are attracted to these disturbed environments (hence "disturbed taxa").

Using modern reference guides, we identified those animals that prefer or thrive in disturbed areas (Table 2.3). We follow VanDerwarker's (2006, 159-160) definition of "disturbance taxa" as those animals that prefer secondary growth, forest-edges, agricultural fields, and urban or suburban areas. We excluded dogs, as they are domesticated and can tolerate a variety of environments, and aquatic animals. Using MNI estimates, we compare the percentage of MNI of disturbance taxa (MNI = 63) to the total MNI for identified taxa (MNI = 115). This shows that disturbance taxa account for nearly 55% of the animals identified at Rutherford-Kizer. While this data analysis is based on one measure (MNI), it appears that the residents of Rutherford-Kizer were clearing primary forests for agricultural and construction purposes, and in turn exploiting those animals that are attracted to these newly disturbed environments. For future research it would be useful to see if there are any changes in the quantity of disturbance taxa through time.

DISTURBANCE FAUNA	MNI	%MNI
Opossum	2	1.74
Striped skunk	2	1.74
Raccoon	1	0.87
Elk/wapiti	2	1.74
White-tailed deer	24	20.87
Woodchuck	1	0.87
Eastern gray squirrel	5	4.35
Eastern fox squirrel	7	6.09
Chipmunk	1	0.87
Eastern cottontail rabbit	2	1.74
Canada goose	1	0.87
Bobwhite	2	1.74
Wild turkey	9	7.83
American crow	1	0.87
Passenger pigeon	1	0.87
Bobwhite quail	2	1.74
Total	63	54.78

Table 2.3. Regional Disturbance Fauna Identified at Rutherford-Kizer.

DISCUSSION OF ANIMAL EXPLOITATION PATTERNS AND CONCLUSIONS REGARDING THE GARDEN-HUNTING MODEL

The residents of Rutherford-Kizer relied on agriculture as a main component to their subsistence system, which is indicated by the presence of maize and beans in the paleoethnobotanical assemblage (Shea and Moore 2001). That agriculture was taking place at or near Rutherford-Kizer, and given that what we call a "site" today was "a substantial fortified town...approximately 14-15 acres in size, including one large platform mound and several low structural mounds" (Moore and Smith 2001, 235), a reasonable conclusion is that land would have been cleared for house garden plots, cultivated fields, construction, and fuel. These newly-created disturbed and forest-edge environments set up new areas for those animals that prefer such habitats, which in turn would have made them easy prey for the humans responsible for managing these areas.

Breitburg characterized the Rutherford-Kizer faunal assemblage "by a substantial reliance on animal species taken within or along forest edges and open forest habitats. Hunting white-tailed deer was a primary means by which Rutherford-Kizer residents obtained meat" (Breitburg and Moore 2001, 133). Our present analysis of the zooarchaeological data also indicates that white-tailed deer was the primary prey animal; and while the assemblage is rich, the Shannon-Weaver values indicate one or a few taxa were more heavily exploited overall.

The majority of the faunal assemblage comprises terrestrial animals, suggesting that the residents of Rutherford-Kizer relied most heavily on these animals. The greater number of terrestrial animals is in line with Linares' model for garden hunting. Linares (1976) suggests that as people become more involved in agricultural activities, they expend less of their efforts on fishing and more on hunting those terrestrial animals that are attracted to the disturbed areas. In addition, it appears that the residents of Rutherford-Kizer were able to practice a selective hunting strategy, as shown by the overwhelming number of white-tailed deer remains in the faunal assemblage.

Interestingly, Bruce Smith (1975) proposed a model of animal exploitation for Mississippian sites in the Mississippi River Valley, in which he characterized these strategies as targeting white-tailed deer, migratory birds, and seasonal fish use. While it is generally accepted that people living in Middle Tennessee did not have the same access to migratory bird populations as their counterparts to the west, they did have access to aquatic animals. It may be that one reason the relative quantities of aquatic taxa are low is their seasonal use. While we cannot say with certainty the degree to which tasks may have been divided based on gender, the reliance on agriculture as the primary means of subsistence surely would have limited time for all residents who participated in food production. Regardless, we feel confident that the residents of Rutherford-Kizer were practicing a selective pattern of garden hunting.

ACKNOWLEDGMENTS

We are grateful to Margaret Williamson Huber for inviting us to contribute a paper to this volume. This paper is a revised version of the paper presented as part of the symposium "Old Collections, New Questions: The re-evaluation of archaeological collections from Middle Tennessee," organized by Tanya Peres and Teresa Ingalls. Our symposium was organized to highlight the new and exciting types of research that were being conducted using existing archaeological collections.

WORKS CITED

Arizona Governor's Archaeology Advisory Commission. 2006. "The Archaeological Curation Crisis in Arizona." http://www.pr. state.az.us/partnerships/shpo/Curation%20Crisis%20 Executive.pdf.

Grayson, Donald K. 1984. *Quantitative Zooarchaeology*. New York: Academic Press.

Guttman, E.B.A.. 2005. "Midden Cultivation in Prehistoric Britain: Arable Crops in Gardens." *World Archaeology* 37(2):224-239.

Johnston, Robert. 2005. "A Social Archaeology of Garden Plots in the Bronze Age of Northern and Western Britain." *World Archaeology* 37(2):211-223.

Linares, Olga F. 1976. "'Garden Hunting' in the American Tropics." *Human Ecology* 4(4):331-349.

Moore, Michael C., and Kevin E. Smith. 2001. *Archaeological Excavations at the Rutherford Kizer Site: A Mississippian Mound Center in Sumner County, Tennessee.* Nashville: Research Series No. 13, Division of Archaeology. Tennessee Department of Environment and Conservation.

Naughton-Treves, Lisa, Jose Luis Mena, Adrain Treves, Nora Alvarez, and Volker Christian Radeloff. 2003. "Wildlife Survival Beyond Park Boundaries: The Impact of Slash-and-Burn Agriculture and Hunting on Mammals in Tambopata, Peru." *Conservation Biology* 17(4):1106-1117

Neusius, Sarah W. 1996. "Game Procurement Among Temperate Horticulturists: The Case for Garden Hunting by the Dolores Anasazi." In *Case Studies in Environmental Archaeology*, edited by Elizabeth J. Reitz, Lee A. Newsom, and Sylvia J. Scudder, 273-288. New York: Plenum Press.

Peres, Tanya M. 2006. "Mississippian Animal Exploitation in Middle Tennessee: A Case Study from the Castalian Springs Site (40SU14)." Paper presented at the 63rd Annual Meeting of the Southeastern Archaeological Conference, November, Little Rock, Arkansas.

Peres, T. M., with contributions by R. Matt Byron and Alison M. Hadley. 2005. *Analysis of Zooarchaeological Remains from the Fewkes Site (40WM1), Tennessee.* Technical Report No. 549. Lexington: Program for Archaeological Research, University of Kentucky.

Reitz, Elizabeth J., and Elizabeth S. Wing. 1999. *Zooarchaeology.* Cambridge: Cambridge University Press.

Shea, Andrea B., and Michael C. Moore. 2001. "Floral Remains." In *Archaeological Excavations at the Rutherford Kizer Site: A Mississippian Mound Center in Sumner County, Tennessee,* edited by M. C. Moore and K. E. Smith, 135-140. Research Series No. 13, Division of Archaeology. Nashville: Tennessee Department of Environment and Conservation.

Scarry, Margaret C., and John F. Scarry. 2005. "Native American 'Garden Agriculture' in Southeastern North America." *World Archaeology* 37(2):259-274.

Smith, Bruce D. 1975. *Middle Mississippian Exploitation of Animal Populations.* Anthropological Papers No. 57. Ann Arbor: University of Michigan Museum of Anthropology.

Stankowski, Cindy, 1998. "The Curation Crisis: Can We Afford the Future?" *Minerva Online* I(1), http://www.sfsu.edu/~museumst/minerva/stankow.html.

VanDerwarker, Amber M. 2006. *Farming, Hunting, and Fishing in the Olmec World.* Austin: University of Texas Press.

White, T. E. 1953. "A Method of Calculating the Dietary Percentage of Various Food Animals Utilized by Aboriginal Peoples." *American Antiquity* 18(4):396-398.

Remembering New Deal Archaeology in the Southeast: A Legacy in Museum Collections

Lynne P. Sullivan, Bobby R. Braly, Michaelyn S. Harle,
and Shannon D. Koerner
Frank H. McClung Museum, The University of Tennessee

On October 29, 1929, the stock market of the United States crashed. This day, also known as Black Tuesday, signaled not only the beginning of the Great Depression, but a new era in southern archaeology. Federal relief programs, hailed as the "New Deal," were initiated by the Franklin D. Roosevelt administration throughout the United States during the 1930s and '40s to employ millions of workers left jobless by the economic collapse (Figure 3.1). The New Deal pro-

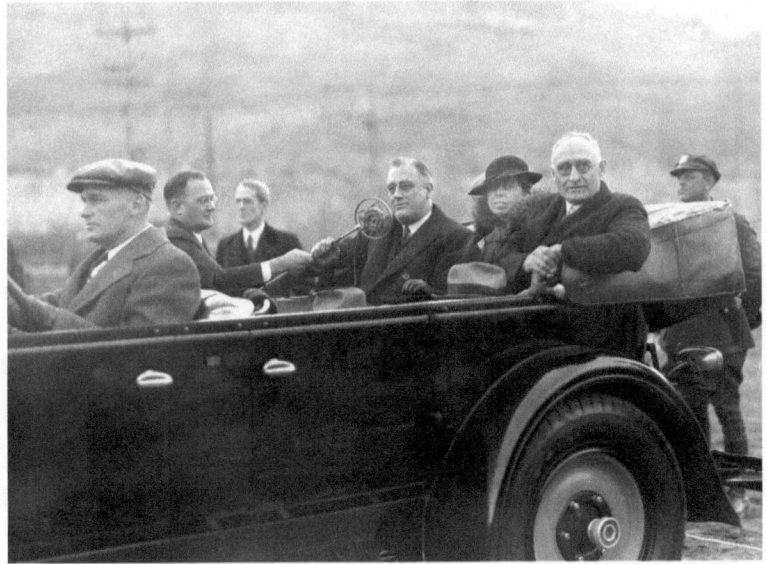

Figure 3.1. Franklin D. Roosevelt, Eleanor Roosevelt, and Arthur E. Morgan (first chairman of the Tennessee Valley Authority) visit Norris Dam construction. (Photo courtesy of the Tennessee Valley Authority.)

grams required a majority of funds to be used for labor so as to provide aid directly to the unemployed through "make work" programs.

Archaeology became a prime vehicle for allocation of money because it was labor-intensive and required little more than paper, pencils, shovels, and wheelbarrows to go along with the manpower funded by the New Deal programs (Lyon 1996; Fagette 1996) (Figure 3.2). The South in particular provided an excellent location for New Deal archaeology projects because of its year-round temperate climate and deeply buried sites that required a lot of labor to excavate. The location of many of these sites in the rural South and Appalachia also made strategic economic sense. In many southern rural areas, poverty was endemic even before the Depression; and with the impact of the Wall Street collapse on southern economies, local governments could scarcely provide relief to the rural poor (Fagette 1996).

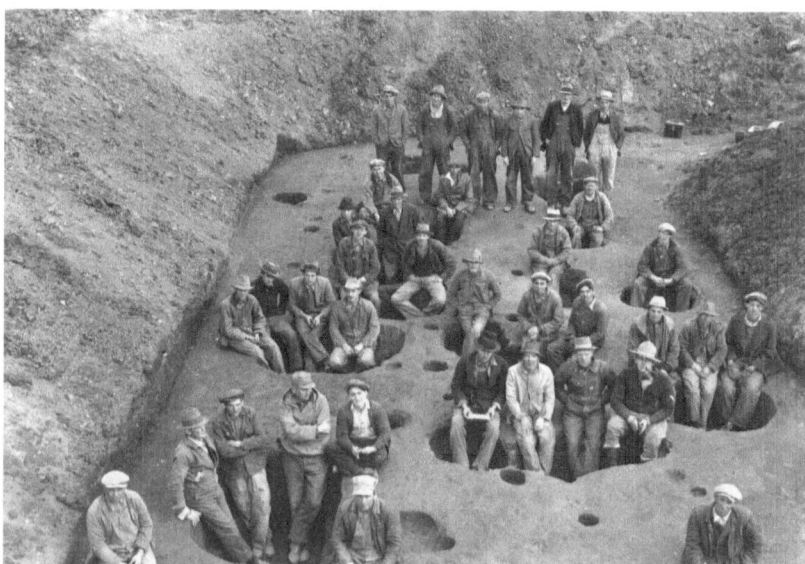

Figure 3.2. New Deal-era crew at the Fains Island Site (40JE1), Jefferson County, Tennessee. (Photo courtesy of the Frank. H. McClung Museum, University of Tennessee.)

The New Deal archaeological projects not only provided jobs and monetary support for needy southern families, but made long-lasting impacts within the fields of archaeology and anthropology. The establishment of museums and anthropology departments at southern universities was one significant result of these federal projects. A second was the training ground federal relief programs provided for a generation of influential archaeologists. A third was the generation of vast collections, which continue to be curated by several university museums whose genesis is itself tied to the New Deal projects. These collections chronicle not only the lifeways of the prehistoric American Indians whose histories are embedded in the excavated materials, but also people of the Great Depression era, including the archaeologists who directed the projects, the rural poor employed on field crews, and a mix of white- and pink-collar laboratory workers.

The New Deal-era archaeological collections thus are a legacy of life in the South for many groups at many points in time. Following a brief survey of the New Deal programs that involved archaeology, this article first discusses connections among the New Deal archaeological collections, southern museums and anthropology departments, and the development of modern archaeology. It then introduces the anthropologists and everyday people who directed and worked on these projects and highlights their contributions. Finally, it provides an idea of ongoing research about ancient Native Americans that is being conducted with the New Deal collections, and then concludes with a summary of current efforts to preserve and make these collections accessible to a wide audience.

The main focus here is on the New Deal archaeological projects conducted in conjunction with the construction of Tennessee Valley Authority (TVA) reservoirs because of the enormous scope of these projects. The collections from these projects are curated by the Alabama Museum of Natural History (AMNH) at the University of

Alabama (UA), the William S. Webb Museum at the University of Kentucky (UK), and the Frank H. McClung Museum at the University of Tennessee (UT). As part of the increasing effort to make these collections more accessible to many audiences, digital identification (DID) numbers are provided for relevant photographic images (in addition to those images published here). These photographs can be viewed on the Internet in a searchable archive of original images from the New Deal-era archaeology collections that are curated by the McClung and Webb Museums, and the AMNH.[1] The url for the website is: diglib.lib.utk.edu/wpa/index.htm.

THE NEW DEAL ARCHAEOLOGY PROGRAMS IN THE SOUTH

New Deal excavations across the South provided jobs for numerous people, but this was highly variable between states. Nine states received approximately sixty percent of New Deal funds for archaeological research. These were Alabama, Arkansas, Florida, Georgia, Kentucky, Louisiana, Oklahoma, Tennessee, and Texas (Milner and Smith 1986, 13). Milner and Smith (1986, 62) estimate 281 people a month were employed for archaeology projects in Kentucky at the peak of New Deal activities. In contrast, South Carolina did not participate in any New Deal archaeological projects.

Although many programs existed, five became the primary providers of New Deal archaeological funding. The detailed structure and form of these enormous bureaucratic programs can best be understood as a two-pronged approach. The Federal Emergency Relief Administration (FERA), Civil Works Administration (CWA), and the Works Progress Administration (WPA) were essentially changing forms of one program directed toward providing jobs for the unemployed, while the Civilian Conservation Corps (CCC) and TVA were focused on natural resource development and regional development, respectively.

The first of the New Deal programs to perform archaeology was the CCC. These archaeology projects were located across the United States, but at smaller scales than later New Deal programs. The CCC was established on March 19, 1933, with the primary focus of providing employment to young men who were required to live in camps with strict rules of work hours and assignments, coupled with meal schedules and recreation activities. Requirements often were placed on workers to send a portion of their earnings home to their families. CCC labor was used at the Jamestown site in Virginia, one of the few historical archaeology sites investigated during the New Deal (Lyon 1996, 188). Recently archaeologists have excavated some of the CCC camps to learn more about the lives of the people that were part of these projects (Smith 2001).

The second New Deal program that funded archaeology was FERA, which granted 500 million dollars directly to states (Lyon 1996, 27). The Marksville site in Louisiana, sponsored by FERA, was probably the first New Deal archeology project, even though the CCC was established before FERA (Lyon 1996, 28). The Marksville project, run by Frank Setzler, proved to the Washington bureaucracy that archaeology could be a prime candidate for relief aid; but generally, the FERA program was a failure and did not alleviate the national unemployment crisis. President Roosevelt then signed the Emergency Relief Appropriation Act in 1935 which allocated $4.88 billion to the relief effort and created the WPA. Archaeology jobs under the WPA far outnumbered those of the previous FERA and CWA programs.

The final New Deal program to sponsor archaeology was the TVA, which was established in 1933. TVA was created not only to provide jobs for the unemployed, but also to improve navigation, control flooding, and generate cheap electricity in an area that was struggling with the effects of the Great Depression. Cash income in the

Mid-South averaged less than $100 per year per family (Lyon 1996, 37-38) in portions of Tennessee, Virginia, North Carolina, Georgia, Alabama, and Mississippi. Ten of the forty-nine TVA reservoirs of today were constructed between 1933 and 1945, nine of which were surveyed for archaeological sites.

The previously discussed New Deal programs, such as the CWA and WPA, provided wages for the archaeological workers during TVA projects. Often, the term "WPA" is used to describe New Deal programs in general; however, in this article the terms "New Deal," "WPA," and "TVA" are used relatively interchangeably since these programs were often interwoven, as was the case with TVA projects utilizing WPA and CWA labor.

RELATIONSHIPS BETWEEN NEW DEAL ARCHAEOLOGY PROJECTS, SOUTHERN MUSEUMS, AND ANTHROPOLOGY DEPARTMENTS

The establishment of several southern museums and anthropology departments was connected to New Deal programs. The archaeology program at the AMNH was greatly expanded in the 1930s by the Wheeler (Webb 1939), Pickwick (Webb and DeJarnette 1942), and Guntersville (Webb and Wilder 1951) reservoir projects that employed CWA labor. The WPA also funded excavations at the Bessemer site in Jefferson County, Alabama (DeJarnette and Wimberly 1941), and numerous sites in Baldwin, Mobile, and Clarke counties (Knight 1993). The Webb Museum at the University of Kentucky (UK), the McClung Museum at the University of Tennessee (UT), and the Louisiana Museum of Natural History at Louisiana State University (LSU) all can trace their roots to WPA excavations.

The William S. Webb Museum of Anthropology was founded in 1931 and, as is discussed below, was named for one of the principal architects of New Deal archaeology. The Museum of Anthropology was founded by Webb and his collaborator William D. Funkhouser specifically to house the multitude of artifacts and excavation re-cords generated by New Deal-era projects in Kentucky; it was later named to honor Webb. At the time of the New Deal projects, UK was one of the few universities in the United States to have an indepen-dent department of anthropology.

Although not officially established until the 1960s, the creation of the Frank H. McClung Museum was a direct result of advocacy by New Deal-era archaeologists at UT for a museum to curate col-lections from the TVA/WPA projects. The Department of Anthro-pology at UT originally was established as the "Division of Anthro-pology" in the history department. Collections from excavations by UT archaeologists in the Chickamauga (Lewis, Lewis and Sullivan 1995), Watts Bar, Norris (Webb 1938), Douglas, Ft. Loudon, and Kentucky Lake reservoirs are curated at the McClung Museum, as are collections from several other New Deal projects, including the Ft. Loudoun and Chota sites in the Little Tennessee River Valley and the Chucalissa site near Memphis.

Excavations at the Chucalissa site established a WPA-constructed park that includes a reconstructed Mississippian period village; the remnants of an earthen platform mound are enclosed by a build-ing and are visible to visitors. The museum at the park is named for Charles H. Nash, the supervisor of New Deal-era excavations who continued research at the site in the post-Depression era.

While not part of the TVA reservoir projects, the Louisiana WPA archaeological project was one of the largest and most influential, especially the surveys and excavations that were conducted in the Lower Mississippi River Valley (Lyon 1996, 78-95). The collections from this work now form the major archaeological holdings of the Louisiana Museum of Natural History at LSU.

In addition to the genesis and growth of museums and anthropology departments across the South, New Deal programs also led to
the creation of a regional archaeology conference. The Southeastern
Archaeological Conference (or SEAC) was created in 1938 as a platform for archaeologists to report on New Deal excavations, discuss
findings, synthesize broad trends, and coordinate regional efforts
[DID uam02009].

NEW DEAL ARCHAEOLOGY COLLECTIONS AS CHRONICLES OF THE DEVELOPMENT OF MODERN ARCHAEOLOGY

One of the most prominent implications of the New Deal funding on
archaeology was the 1938 Society for American Archaeology meetings. Almost every paper at these meetings reported results of WPA
projects. New Deal achievements also formalized archaeology in the
South and created a stepping-stone for federal archaeology programs
today. William Haag (1985, 278), in his reflections on WPA archaeology, wrote, "New Deal archaeology did more than produce archaeologists. It took Americanists forever away from an ethnogenetic
view of our prehistory. It developed our thinking to where even a gas
pipeline could not be strung across the nation without considering
the damage to the prehistoric record."

The artifacts and records generated by New Deal-era archaeological projects are primary documentation not only of archaeological sites but also of the innovations in archaeology fostered by New
Deal projects. As noted above, the New Deal projects employed new
techniques and methods, some learned from Chicago field schools
and then altered to fit southern sites and the New Deal crews. These
procedures enabled the collection of new kinds of data, which led to
new understandings of prehistory. These systematic field techniques
and the related documentation provided by maps, field records,
preliminary reports, photographs, artifacts, and catalogs form an

irreplaceable record that makes the collections derived from the New Deal-era excavations extraordinarily useful for ongoing research because they provide a depth and span of information on the ancient Native American cultures of the South that cannot be duplicated.

Stratigraphic excavation techniques that emphasized vertical control were not widely used in the South before the 1930s. The lack of vertical control led to a poor understanding of prehistoric time depth. The stratigraphic techniques used in the New Deal investigations added new perspective to the temporal development of Native American cultures [DID fhm01391, wsw04571]. The collections include carefully drawn profiles of mound and site stratigraphy as well as photographs and manuals showing the techniques used to expose the deposits [DID wsw02122, fhm01517]. The mound excavated by WPA crews at the Hiwassee Island site in the Chickamauga Reservoir near Chattanooga, Tennessee was one of the first in the eastern United States to be investigated using the "peeling" technique which exposed entire horizontal surfaces or summits (Willey and Sabloff 1974, 130). (See Figure 3.3).

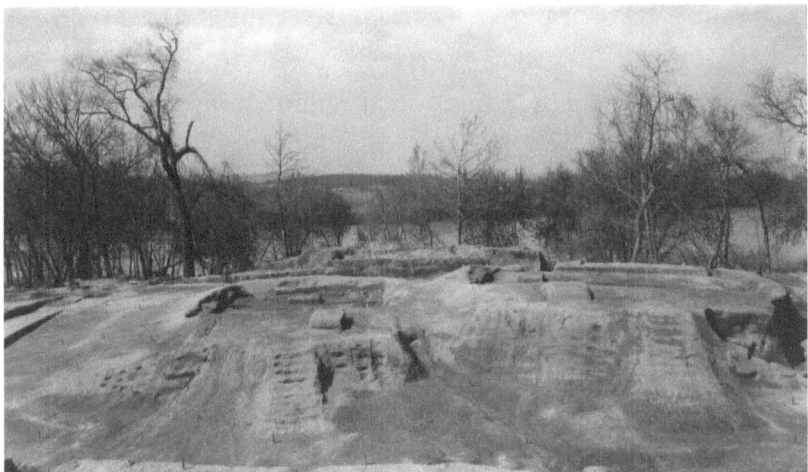

Figure 3.3. Example of "mound-peeling" technique used at the Hiwassee Island Site (40MG31), Meigs County, Tennessee. (Photo courtesy of the Frank. H. Mc-Clung Museum, University of Tennessee.)

Other New Deal innovations included photography as a standard recording technique and the use of standardized data collection forms, including excavation unit, feature, and burial records that required those who completed them to collect certain categories of data systematically, in a uniform fashion. This innovation not only aided in the management of large WPA crews, but it also made it easier to use the records because of the consistent format of the records. Grid systems with standardized square units were employed in surveying, mapping, trenching, and excavating sites, and detailed maps were made of the excavations. Artifacts were carefully cataloged with field specimen numbers keyed into this systematic provenience system.

Material culture, previously relegated merely to trait lists, was carefully studied in WPA laboratories. Changes in subsistence practices, ceramics, and other material culture began to be discussed in terms of culture change. The excavation of entire sites, not only mounds, provided new interpretive potential for settlement patterns, including site plans and structure patterns. Houses, storage pits, and other features, relatively undocumented prior to the 1930s, became important components of archaeological data in New Deal archaeology [DID fhm00210]. Some WPA crews conducted experiments the better to understand prehistoric architecture. At the Thompson Village Site in Henry County, Tennessee, WPA workers reconstructed a prehistoric house based on the archaeological structure pattern (Sullivan 2007a) [DID fhm01027]. Later, similar reconstructions were made at the Chucalissa site near Memphis as part of an interpretation for the site museum (Nash 1968; Sullivan 2007a, 131-132).

Innovative interpretive perspectives allowed artifacts and archaeological deposits to be placed in human behavioral contexts and made it possible for southern museums to display artifacts and provide interpretations. In contrast, before the New Deal projects, archaeology in the South was dominated largely by amateur archaeologists and curiosity seekers. Professional archaeologists conducted excavations in the South before 1930, but many of these projects focused on obtaining exhibition-quality specimens for northern museums. These specimens, rarely a representative sample, did little to promote understanding of large-scale cultural traditions and the day-to-day lives of prehistoric Native Americans.

THE NEW DEAL ARCHAEOLOGISTS AS SEEN IN THE PHOTOGRAPHIC ARCHIVES

The numerous New Deal projects employed hundreds, possibly thousands, of people to excavate archaeological sites in the South [DID wsw01993, uam01107]. Many of the archaeologists who were employed as supervisors to run these projects became well known in the field, but the names of most of those who worked on the large excavation crews and in the laboratories are not known. The little that is known about these men and women comes mainly from brief comments in archaeological field reports and accounts from the archaeological field directors. The extensive photographic record made by the supervisors and workers does, however, provide a visual documentation of the important role that everyday individuals outside the archaeological discipline, including disenfranchised groups (e.g., the rural poor, women, and African Americans), played in these projects. Within this collection, hundreds of photographs document the field and laboratory workers performing their assigned duties, as well as the field laborers' living and working conditions. In most instances these photographs are the only documentation of these workers.

As noted above, this photograph collection is now accessible to the general public on the Internet, an arrangement that allows the descendants of these men and women to witness the contributions their ancestors made in preserving the past. Most of the descriptions of these photographs are unaccompanied by names of those pictured. Finding out more about these people is difficult with this crucial information lacking. One of the desired outcomes of the online photo project is that more stories of these women and men will come to light and that the names and experiences of many of these individuals may be documented.

It is important to note that gender and race were often factors in the type of employment one could have on the New Deal projects. Jurisdiction of women's work in the WPA in general fell under the branch of the "Women's and Professional Projects" (Claassen 1999). For the most part, these jobs consisted of domestic activities in the public domain; but inequality, especially in the southern states, characterized the allocation of relief work between white and black women. The distribution of work for archaeology projects also reflected gender, class, and racial lines. As a result, many African American women were assigned to "pick and shovel" jobs (Whalen 2008). African American women also contributed to laboratory work [DID uam02346], but they were not restricted from fieldwork as were white women. Educated women in general, and especially white women, were confined to laboratory and museum projects [DID uam01974]. Harriet Smith, a University of Chicago graduate student in archaeology, was one of the few women, if not the only one, allowed to supervise a WPA excavation. It took her four years to convince the WPA archaeology bureaucracy that she was capable of doing this job. She supervised the excavation of a mound at the Cahokia site in Illinois (Claassen 1999, 109-111; Sullivan 1999, 64-65).

THE FIELD SUPERVISORS

Each state that received New Deal funding for archaeology eventually had its own organization to manage the projects. The TVA projects also had a central administration through TVA. One of the most important figures in New Deal archaeology was Major William S. Webb, who served as director of the TVA archaeological program, initially oversaw the TVA projects in Tennessee, and was responsible for New Deal-era excavations at many sites in Kentucky that used both WPA and CCC labor (Figure 3.4).

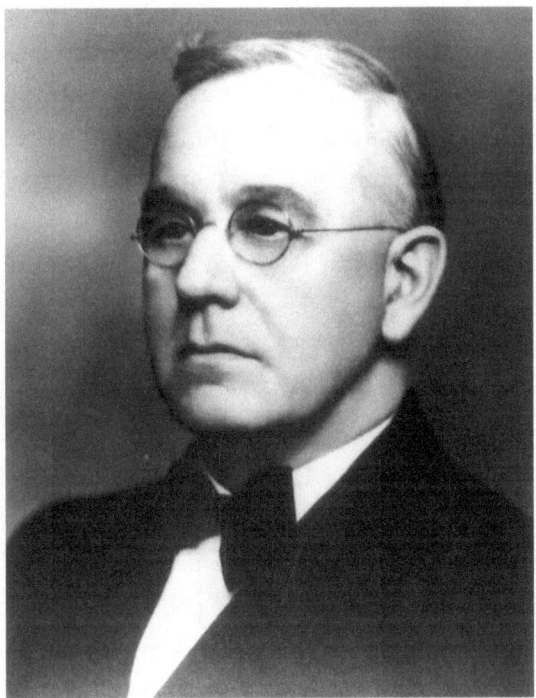

Figure 3.4. William S. Webb. (Photo courtesy of the William S. Webb Museum of Anthropology, University of Kentucky.)

Webb was selected as the Director of Archaeology for TVA after
W.C. McKern of the Milwaukee Public Museum refused the offer
(Lyon 1996, 40). Although Webb was appointed chairman of the Anthropology Department upon its creation at UK, he was previously a
professor of physics. His lack of formal training in archaeology was
a point of criticism, and by some accounts his field techniques were
horrid (Jennings 1994); but his passion, leadership, and organiza-
tional skills largely made up for these shortcomings (Jennings 1994;
Lyon 1996; Haag 1985).

Thomas M. N. Lewis (Figure 3.5) replaced Webb as director of
TVA archaeology in Tennessee in 1935, and Webb headed back to
Kentucky to direct projects in his home state (Webb and Haag 1939,
1940, 1947a,b). A graduate of Princeton, Lewis was recommended
to Webb by McKern, and he was hired originally by Webb to direct
the fieldwork at the first TVA archaeological projects on the Norris
Reservoir in Tennessee (Lyon 1996, 40; Sullivan 1999, 67-68). All of
the New Deal work in Tennessee was subsequently run through UT
after Lewis established the archaeology program there. Differences
between Lewis and Webb revolved around how to manage cultural
resources in an area that spanned several states and where to focus
funding. Webb preferred the larger regional approach and spend-
ing money on labor; Lewis preferred the state approach. At the same
time, Lewis was quickly realizing the daunting task of analyzing,
curating, and publishing on the large collections produced by the
excavations, and he preferred to spend money on a lab and necessary
supplies (Lyon 1996, 144; Sullivan 1999). Lewis oversaw WPA/TVA
archaeological work in the Chickamauga, Watts Bar, Kentucky Lake,
Ft. Loudoun, and Douglas reservoirs, as well as the Chucalissa site
near Memphis.

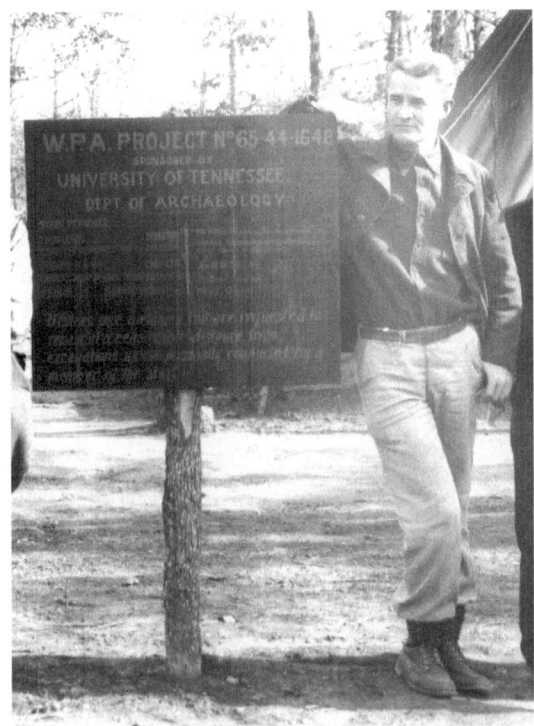

Figure 3.5. Thomas M. N. Lewis. (Photo courtesy of the Frank. H. McClung Museum, University of Tennessee.)

In Alabama, David L. DeJarnette oversaw the large-scale excavations sponsored by TVA and the CWA on the Tennessee River in the Pickwick, Wheeler, and Guntersville basins between 1934 and 1939 (Webb and DeJarnette 1942, 1948a, 1948b) (Figure 3.6). DeJarnette was a "loaner" from the AMNH to TVA to supervise these excavations (Knight 1993). Alabama was a leader in archaeological research from the beginning of the twentieth century, and DeJarnette had joined the museum staff in 1929 as a full-time archaeologist although he was an electrical engineer by education. DeJarnette went on to assume the direction of Mound State Monument in 1953, received his

Master's degree in archaeology in 1958 from UA, and was appointed to the faculty in 1956. He conducted twenty field schools between 1957 and 1975, training a "generation of archaeologists, many of whom practice the craft today" (Knight 1993, 623).

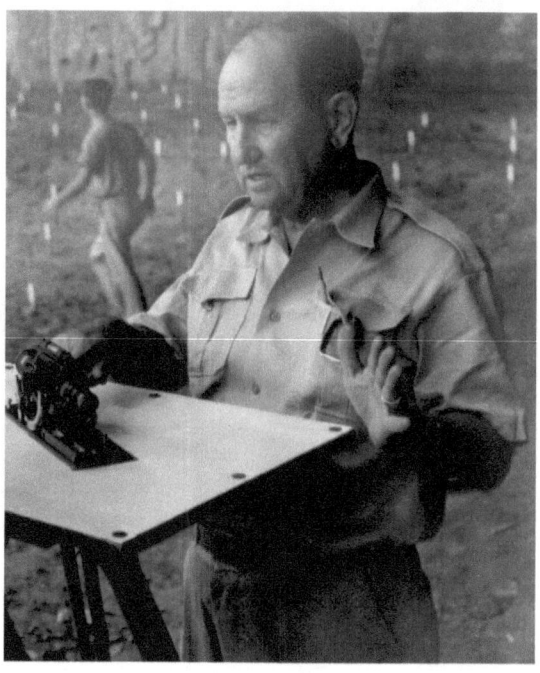

Figure 3.6. David. L. DeJarnette. (Photo courtesy of the Alabama Museum of Natural History, University of Alabama.)

The lack of formal training among archaeologists working on New Deal-era projects initially hindered excavation organization and final reporting (Lyon 1996, 23). For example, Webb, who had no formal training in archaeology, resisted establishing laboratories and structured his archaeological reports as a summary of artifact descriptions and site traits (e.g., Webb 1938). This situation changed somewhat with the influx of trained archaeologists to the WPA projects. By 1938 the WPA archaeological programs included about 200 archaeologists. A significant number of these young field supervisors were alumni of the University of Chicago field school under the direction of the famous anthropologist Faye-Cooper Cole. These ambitious, highly motivated graduate and undergraduate students in archaeology supervised the large numbers of unskilled laborers. The experience they gained during the WPA excavations would be fundamental to their training. They became the next generation of archaeologists and, like DeJarnette in Alabama, directly or indirectly trained many of the modern archaeologists of today.

Lessons and techniques learned from the University of Chicago field schools were applied to southern New Deal excavations and molded to fit southern projects. New excavation methods and techniques coupled with refined anthropological theory produced some of the most important archaeological research and collections in the region to date. The scientific methods that Cole taught are a major reason for the lasting importance of these collections for research.

Field supervisors such as George Neumann, Jesse Jennings, Stuart Neitzel, Charles Nash, James Ford, William Haag, and Charles Fairbanks would go on to have illustrious careers in archaeology (Haag 1985; Jennings 1994; Taylor 2008) [DID fhm00931]. While many may have started their education at the University of Chicago, their real training was through the WPA. Many supervisors describe showing up for the first day of work with little prior experience—only a field school—to face hundreds of untrained men waiting to be told what to do (Jennings 1996; Haag 1985; Walker 1994). Although these professional archaeologists were not employed directly by the WPA per se, in many ways they also were on relief. As one field supervisor, John Elliot, said, "This was the only opportunity I had to practice my profession. It looked like a lost cause...during the start of the Depression. Farming was bad enough, but archaeology was worse" (Kentucky Heritage Council 2002).

THE ARCHAEOLOGICAL FIELD LABORERS

Laborers worked year-round, often in bad conditions. In the winter months, crews set fires in barrels to keep warm and soften the
ground. During the summer, they were confronted by occasional
flooding (Kentucky Heritage Council 2002). Laborers carried out
excavations under severe time restrictions while the threat of inun-
dation worried at their heels. A member of one Douglas Reservoir
field project describes working as the floodwaters began to come in
(Andrew H. Whiteford, personal communication 2002). Living conditions were rustic, to say the least [DID fhm01867]. Workers slept in
tents or in temporary shacks [DID fhm01451, fhm00932, fhm01505].
For some excavations in the Chickamauga Reservoir, the crew slept
in house boats, which were merely corrugated-tin-covered sheds on
ancient leaky barges (Jennings 1994).

Laborers were not always happy with these conditions or with the
pay scale. Jesse Jennings (1994, 86-87) recounts an amusing tale of
an especially ornery crew of former union coal miners from Soddy,
Tennessee, who were employed in the Chickamauga Basin. From the
start the workers formed a "grievance committee" and constantly
threatened to strike for better pay and working conditions. They
eventually raised enough money to send someone to Washington
to plead their case, but the man they selected absconded with all of
their money.

A field manual for the Division of Anthropology at the University
of Tennessee provides some insight regarding the division of labor
of the New Deal workers: the general foremen assisted the archaeologist in charge; house and burial foremen supervised the work of
house and burial crews [DIDfhm00645]; measure men were skilled
with measuring rods and plumb bobs [DID fhm00281, fhm01856];
and the laundry crews were responsible for washing artifacts [DID
fhm01859] (Lewis, Lewis, and Sullivan 1995, 605-609). On the

assignment to the laundry crew, Lewis writes, "the men selected for this work should have a reputation for honesty, and it will be advisable, where possible, to select men who are physically unfit to perform hard labor" (Lewis, Lewis, and Sullivan 1995, 607). Field excavators were divided into select categories such as shovel men who were paid 30 cents an hour, trowel men who were paid a little more, and wheelbarrow men. In the manual, Lewis recommended, "those who have a criminal record should be assigned to wheelbarrows or other work which will provide them least opportunity to steal artifacts" (Lewis, Lewis, and Sullivan 1995, 608). Laborers who were quick learners and especially adept excavators were promoted to general foreman or house and burial foreman.

Fears about the potential disadvantages of using unskilled laborers were mostly unwarranted. In fact, some field innovations developed during the WPA may not have come from the lead archaeologists but from the untrained workers. As one field supervisor, John Elliot, recounts, "[these laborers] were used to working in old-fashioned coalmines on their knees with picks and shovels. In other words they were used to working with tools. They were dexterous and ingenious in solving little problems such as making fine tools and blowing dowels to dust away nooks and crannies...not only were they ingenious, they were hard workers" (Kentucky Heritage Council 2002). As a whole, many field supervisors would describe the New Deal laborers as "hardworking," "cautious," and "enthusiastic of their finds," who quickly "caught the spirit of mystery and interest of the work" (Fagette 1996, 30; Jennings 1994: Kentucky Heritage Council 2002).

Field supervisors taught these men archaeological excavation techniques, while the New Deal laborers taught some of these young middle-class academics about rural southern culture. Lead archaeologists had to quickly learn southern Appalachian vernacular: "poke" for bag, "stob" for stake, "croker sack" for burlap bag (Jennings 1994, 76). The archaeologist Jesse Jennings fondly recalls that it was because of these New Deal laborers that he went to his first rooster fight, first tasted moonshine, and learned how to square dance (1994, 76-77).

As shown in the photograph collections, laborers represented a cross-section of groups most affected by the Great Depression [DID uam01436, wsw00726]. Many of the workers, especially in the earlier CWA years, tended to be older men who had lost their savings in the Great Depression, and those with disabilities—basically those ill-suited for other New Deal jobs [DID fhm01868]. Other laborers were younger men fresh out of school with no skills and few family responsibilities (Fagette 1996) [DID wsw01325]. Several sites, especially in Kentucky, made use of the CCC, which consisted of entire field crews of extremely young men. At the Town Creek site in North Carolina and the Jonathan Creek site in Kentucky, some crews consisted entirely of boys (Lyon 1996) [DID wsw07312].

There was an especially large labor pool of out-of-work African American men. Political pressure from Washington, D.C., pushed for the employment of African Americans; and, in fact, most archaeological field supervisors had no reservations regarding the employment of these men (Fagette 1996). Many New Deal projects in the South were segregated, and so it is remarkable that many photographs of the archaeological crews show whites and blacks, sometimes including African American women (see below), working alongside each other [DID uam00818, uam01368, uam01578]. In the South in particular, African American men on WPA payrolls were paid substantially less than their white counterparts (Fagette 1996). Whether this was the case for archaeological fieldwork is uncertain. While racist attitudes probably did persist in the field, the depiction of some of these men excavating burials and features suggests that at least some of them were promoted to higher positions in the field hierarchy. The photographic documentation of African American men is especially noteworthy, since their depiction in all facets of New Deal work was often ignored within the popular press (Natonson 1992).

Several sites, including Whitesburg Bridge and Flint River in Alabama, Swift Creek and Irene in Georgia, and Town Creek in North Carolina, also employed African American women as archaeological field workers [DID uam01060, uam01223]. Approximately 160 women were employed on these projects in the states of Alabama and Georgia (Hays-Gilpin 2000). The opportunity to work was a blessing for some of these women, whose husbands were gone or disabled. According to one account, when African American women were turned away from fieldwork because of rules barring women from pushing wheelbarrows, they countered that they could instead tote the soil in baskets on their heads (Claassen 1999; White 1999, 8). The photographs show that even in the field, what was deemed acceptable for women still dictated limitations of what these women could and could not do. Whereas men wore standard field clothes, women were expected to wear dresses as they performed heavy labor [DID uam01232]. Clearly, these women were willing to do whatever it took to feed their families.

A well-documented excavation employing African American women was at the Irene Mound along the Savannah River in Georgia (Claassen 1999; Whalen 2008; see images at: www.sip.armstrong. edu/Irene/Irene.html). Not all of the women employed as field workers at Irene were uneducated workers. Some, such as Gussie Smith and Anna Scott, were educators prior to the Depression. Oral histories of the children of these women indicate that their mothers expressed deep interest in their work at Irene, although some would express misgivings about the excavations of burials. One daughter stated that her lifelong interest in Native American culture was stirred by her mother's experience at Irene. The granddaughter of Hattie Coleman, another worker at Irene, recalled that her grandmother valued her work at Irene as the greatest intellectual stimulation in her adult life (Whalen 2008).

By some accounts, these attitudes about acceptable female roles in archaeology persisted as late as the 1970s. Many woman archaeologists today cannot but view the workers at Irene with a sense of pride and validation. Yet, their presence in the field was in many ways consistent with racial attitudes at the time. Their work in the field represented inequalities in the distribution of jobs and perhaps racist views of African American women as "less respectable" or perhaps not as "feminine" as white (Claassen 1999). Nonetheless, oral histories of the women at Irene Mound suggest pride in their work.

THE LABORATORY WORKERS

Large-scale WPA excavations unearthed millions of artifacts that needed to be analyzed and curated. Laboratory analysis of New Deal collections became important under the direction of Vincenzo Petrullo, who was appointed head anthropologist of the WPA in 1938 (Lyon 1996, 70). He envisioned central state laboratories and implemented this plan first in Birmingham, Alabama, where Eleanor Roosevelt made a visit to see the program (Figure 3.7).

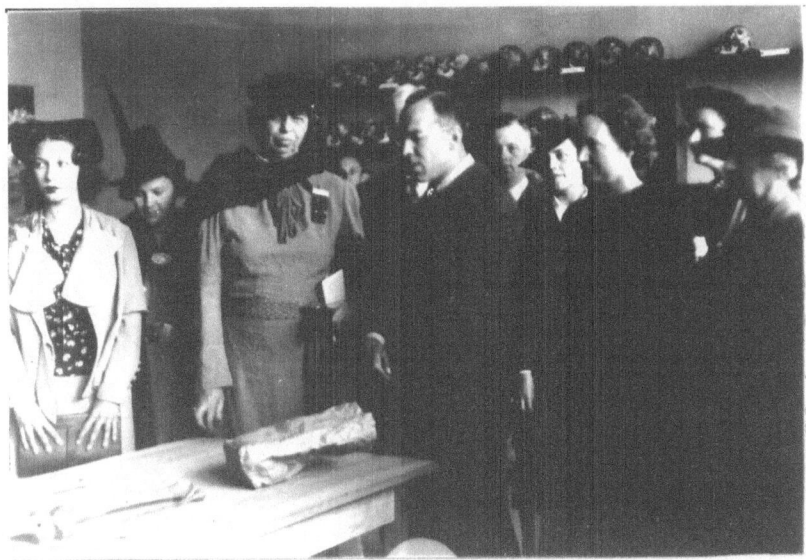

Figure 3.7. Eleanor Roosevelt visits WPA central laboratory in Birmingham, Alabama. (Photo courtesy of the Alabama Museum of Natural History, University of Alabama.)

This lab was the model for later labs in Louisiana, Tennessee, and Texas. The photographs of the laboratory in Alabama show that most labor was done by women, both African American and white (Figure 3.8) [DID uam01971]. There are no photographs of the Tennessee lab, but the records indicate that it employed forty workers and six supervisors at its peak and that more men worked in the lab than did in the Alabama lab. The supervisors included four graduate students in anthropology. Three were University of Chicago students— Madeline Kneberg, J. Joseph Bauxar[2], and Andrew Whiteford—who were the lab director, project ethnohistorian, and artifact analyst, respectively. Alice Hendrick, a University of Michigan student, supervised pottery cataloging and analysis. Doc Goins, an ex-pharmacist, supervised a group of elderly men to clean human bones (Sullivan 1999, 70-71).

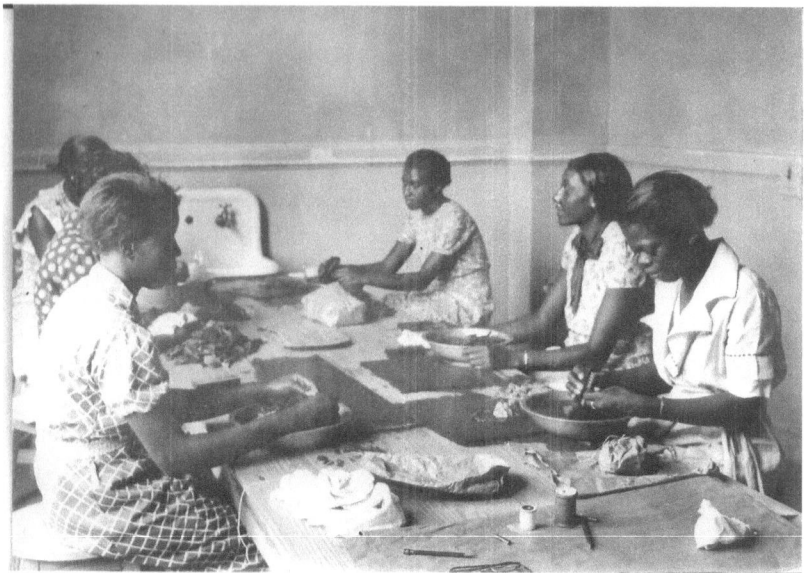

Figure 3.8. African American women cleaning artifacts in the central lab in Birmingham. (Photo courtesy of the Alabama Museum of Natural History, University of Alabama.)

While most male University of Chicago archaeology students got their start as WPA field supervisors, their female counterparts typically were expected to take jobs as laboratory workers and supervisors. Joan Gero (1985, 44) has characterized lab work as "archaeological housework." Perhaps Gero's characterization is a bit unfair, though, because it perpetrates the notion that laboratory processing and analysis are of less consequence than fieldwork. Nonetheless, as we noted previously in reference to Harriet Smith, the role of woman archaeologists was limited by prevailing attitudes of the time.

If laboratory jobs are considered "archaeological housework," then one woman in particular stands out as being an archaeological "domestic goddess." Madeline Kneberg was one of the most influential women in the history of southern archaeology (Powell et al. 2006; Sullivan 1999) (Figure 3.9). Like many other WPA-era archaeologists, Kneberg got her start in anthropology at the University of Chicago, where she was trained mainly in physical anthropology. In 1938, upon the recommendation of Faye-Cooper Cole, Thomas Lewis hired Kneberg to supervise the newly formed UT Archaeological Laboratory in Knoxville. There, she excelled at supervising the processing, analysis, and eventual curation of thousands of artifacts and human remains that were generated by TVA excavations.

Along with Lewis, whom she later married, Kneberg was instrumental in the reconstruction of the prehistoric culture history of Tennessee. Their work in the Chickamauga Basin, especially at the Hiwassee Island site and at the Eva site in Kentucky Lake, produced two of the most important monographs on Tennessee archaeology to come out of this era: *Hiwassee Island: An Archaeological Account of Four Tennessee Indian Peoples* (Lewis and Kneberg 1946) and *Eva: An Archaic Site* (Lewis and Kneberg 1961). This work also propelled archaeology from a purely descriptive phase to one of interpretation. Lewis and Kneberg's interpretations from the Chickamauga Basin and Eva have stood the test of time and remain at the core of modern culture histories for the region (Kimball and Baden 1985; Schroedl 1998; Sullivan 2007b). Throughout her career, Kneberg wrote many articles, including several with Lewis. In some respects her contributions to the field would come to outshine Lewis's work. Her fellow archaeologist Jesse Jennings, whose opinion of Lewis was rather low, went so far as to give Kneberg sole credit for the success of the Eva and Hiwassee Island reports (Jennings 1994, 89).

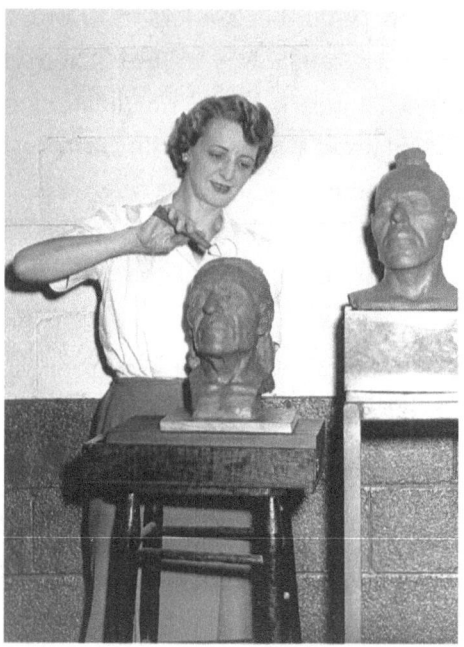

Figure 3.9. Madeline D. Kneberg. (Photo courtesy of the Frank. H. McClung Museum, University of Tennessee.)

In contrast, Florence M. Hawley, one of the first women to appear in the line of female archaeologists in the South, did not receive recognition and appreciation for her work until after her death [DID fhm01866]. Hawley conducted dendrochronological studies in the Norris Basin (1938). Her work was never accepted by the male scientific hierarchy, although modern research has shown that their denial of the validity of her work hindered the growth of dendrochronology in the eastern United States for decades (Nash 1999, 243).

In 2000, the Georgia Women's History Committee of the Georgia Trust for Historic Preservation and the Georgia Commission on Women hosted a ceremony at Spelman College to present Georgia Resolution 985. The Resolution honored and commended the women workers at Irene Mound and Swift Creek for their significant contributions to Georgia historic preservation. Like the women at Irene and Swift Creek, women of all races and classes should be commended for their roles in preserving the cultural heritage of the Southeast. In the face of the limitations imposed on them, women nevertheless managed to change the field of archaeology by establishing proper curatorial and analysis techniques, advancing specialized fields such as dendrochronology and bioarchaeology, and demonstrating that they could do fieldwork just as well as men.

THE NEW DEAL ARCHAEOLOGY COLLECTIONS AS SOURCES FOR NEW STUDIES

Even though the New Deal projects established significant milestones in the conduct of archaeology and interpretation in the United States, the onset of World War II prohibited reporting on many of the massive projects. After the United States became involved in the war in the winter of 1941, labor was no longer a surplus and money was needed elsewhere (Sullivan 1995a, xxv). Except for the Norris Basin report compiled by Webb (1938), no other New Deal-era collections were systematically reported in Tennessee until 1946 (the Hiwassee Island site report) and 1961 (the Eva site report). A comprehensive Chickamauga Basin report was limited to a preliminary publication (Lewis and Kneberg 1941) until an edited form was published in the mid-1990s (Lewis, Lewis, and Sullivan 1995). Reports on projects in other states faced similar fates.

Although the lack of reports for many sites and projects hindered the wide dissemination and incorporation of much information into archaeological interpretations, the collections derived from New Deal-era excavations provide a depth of information on Native Indian cultures that would be difficult to duplicate today. The New Deal-era project directors had to do the best possible job on a tight schedule with meager resources, and they chose to perform very detailed investigations at a few sites instead of obtaining small samples from many sites (Lyon 1996, 143). They focused their attention on large, monumental sites and sites with well-defined stratigraphic records because all archaeological resources in the area of impact would be destroyed (those below the reservoir pool level).

New Deal archaeology in the South recovered millions of artifacts. Valuable information includes not only the artifacts themselves, but also all of the associated contextual information such as photographs, field records, excavation maps, and even preliminary interpretations. As an example of the scope of these projects, the Chickamauga Reservoir project alone generated over a half a million artifacts, and it was responsible for the excavation of thirteen significant mound and village sites. The Chickamauga Basin archaeologists excavated, mapped, and photographed five platform mounds, eight burial mounds, ten villages, 165 structures, nearly two thousand burials, 360,000 pottery sherds, and some 100,000 stone, bone, shell, and copper artifacts (Sullivan 1995, xvii). The Norris Basin project, also in eastern Tennessee, identified and excavated twenty-three archaeological sites. Another highlight of the New Deal projects is the unique information that was collected about previously unknown aspects of American Indian culture. For example, the Eva site in the Kentucky Lake reservoir in western Tennessee would become one of the best examples of Archaic Period (6000-1000 BC) occupation in the South, documenting an extremely long span of human occupation in the region.

The fact that the New Deal collections were made over a half century ago does present some challenges for contemporary researchers. Anthropologists and archaeologists of the early twentieth century asked somewhat different questions than do modern professionals. The New Deal archaeologists did not intentionally collect information pertinent to the organization of technology and subsistence practices, and the New Deal emphasis on chronology-building emphasized collection of formal tools and complete specimens, largely excluding the manufacturing debris and broken tools that now are useful for technological analyses. Today's standard practice of sifting all excavated soils for small artifacts was not practiced in the 1930s, either; nor was flotation, a technique that enables the collection of small bones, seeds, and charcoal. For these reasons, among others discussed below, several kinds of materials were not systematically collected and curated by New Deal archaeologists.

Even though all excavated materials were listed in field and laboratory records, some were not curated in perpetuity. Most decorated ceramic sherds were retained, but many of the plain, undecorated sherds were discarded. Retention of lithic artifacts was limited to tools and not debitage. Animal bones and shells were seldom kept except for formal tools or ornaments. Botanical remains were kept only if they were exceptional samples, such as burned architectural elements or corn cobs. Contrary to most other aspects of New Deal-era excavations, human burials were investigated with more vigor than most other cultural features. Great detail was obtained regarding the sex, age, stature, location, and grave associations of each burial. In fact, the human burial remains and records from New Deal excavations are the basis of much modern research on Native American health and biological diversity.

Although few botanical samples or artifacts were curated, many valuable architectural samples such as intact wooden posts, steps, or rafters were preserved and curated. Dendrochronology, as pioneered by Florence Hawley, is a means of using intact wood to produce absolute dates for archaeological sites. Samples collected in the 1930s for Hawley are proving invaluable today for constructing a regional sequence. Dendrochronology assigns annual growth rings of wood to the exact year of formation; cut dates thus document the years trees were harvested. The application of dendrochronology as an absolute dating technique in archaeology is common in the American Southwest, but it has been more difficult in the Southeast because of preservation issues and difficulties in establishing a prehistoric reference chronology (Koerner, Grissino-Mayer, and Sullivan 2007; Braly et al. 2008). Dendrochronological studies using New Deal-era collections are now yielding promising results for dating late prehistoric sites in the Upper Tennessee Valley, and they may provide a proxy of ancient climate in the region.

New Deal-era investigators also sometimes varied in the quality and organization of their excavations. Working with large labor pools for short amounts of time was a novel situation and, as such, some excavations produced very different data and records than later projects. The earliest work in the Norris Basin in 1934 was not recorded with as much detail as later projects in the Watts Bar and Chickamauga Basin. In some cases, now-outdated excavation strategies used in early excavations significantly complicated interpretive research. For example, the excavation of the Hixon mound (40HA3) in Hamilton County was done entirely in vertical sections (like a loaf of sliced bread) that have confounded attempts to line up the vertical profiles into discernable horizontal surfaces [DID fhm00846]. Nonetheless, the well-defined stratigraphy in this mound has been used to seriate shell gorgets associated with burials (Kneberg 1959; Sullivan 2007b).

Despite these issues, the New Deal-era collections, with their extensive and intensive coverage of major sites, have been useful for answering an array of questions about the past (but there are certainly others). These questions include: (1) socio-political organization; (2) human health and demography (including issues of migration and resource stress); (3) artifacts studies, such as technological and stylistic studies of pottery, bone, stone, and shell tools, and ornaments; (4)

gender relations; (5) the prevalence of warfare as identified through skeletal trauma; and lastly (6) relations among regional groups, including correlates with ethnic boundaries and the extent of interaction spheres in prehistory.

The discussion here focuses on the New Deal collections from Tennessee as examples of the research accomplishments and potential of these materials because these are the collections with which the authors are most familiar (but see Peebles et al. 1981). The Tennessee collections have become a data source for numerous thesis and dissertation projects. New Deal collections housed at the University of Tennessee's Frank H. McClung Museum alone have been the subject of over 65 theses and dissertations. New Deal-era collections have been used extensively in syntheses specific to Tennessee also.

In the Upper Tennessee Valley, James Hatch (1974) used strictly New Deal-era collections to study mortuary practices as a means to interpret societal organization at Middle and Late Mississippian sites (c. AD 1100-1540). He found that not all of these societies were similarly structured, and that the ranking of persons was expressed differently through time. The distinctions between high-status men and women based on burial data raised important questions about the validity of neo-evolutionary models (e.g., Service 1962) in the Southeast. Syntheses in the late 1970s and early 1980s expounded on the Hatch study. Patricia Cole (1975) investigated burial mounds of the Hamilton Complex (Lewis and Kneberg 1946) that were the focus of many New Deal-era excavations along the Upper Tennessee River. Cole found a continuation of egalitarian social organization dating to the Late Woodland-Early Mississippian transition (c. AD 700-1100) (Schroedl 1978). In the early 1980s, Lynne Sullivan investigated Late Mississippian (c. AD 1400-1550) social organization and settlement patterns in southeastern Tennessee. Sullivan (1986, 1987,

1989) studied New Deal-era collections from coeval sites known as the Mouse Creek Phase (Lewis and Kneberg 1946; Lewis, Lewis, and Sullivan 1995). She was able to assert that Mouse Creek culture was significantly different from antecedent Mississippian phases and presented a model of cultural progression in the region (Sullivan 1995, 2007b).

A current research emphasis focuses on using New Deal-era collections to make large-scale comparisons that are lending support to the possibility of sub-regional ethnic and socio-political differences among late prehistoric societies in eastern Tennessee. In 2003, Michaelyn Harle used collections from the Douglas Reservoir in northeastern Tennessee to define Late Mississippian mortuary practices in that area. Her analysis showed that the burial practices in the mound at Fains Island (40JE1) were those of a more egalitarian society than Hatch (1974) proposed for the region. In 2007 Juliette Vogel investigated Late Mississippian mortuary traditions at the Cox Site mound and village (40AN19) in the Norris Reservoir, also in northeastern Tennessee. She discovered a mortuary tradition there similar to that at Fains Island. Comparisons of mortuary practices between northeastern and southeastern Tennessee suggest variation that may correlate with differences in ethnicity (Sullivan and Harle 2010).

Another important research topic has been assessing biological relationships through human physiology. Using multivariate craniofacial measurements, Hugh Berryman (1975) tested Lewis and Kneberg's (1946) hypothesis that Mouse Creek Phase people in southeastern Tennessee actually originated in the Middle Cumberland area of central Tennessee. He was able to find significant affinities between the two physiographic regions that hint at ancestral connections. In 1984, Donna Boyd revisited this model with a study of overall health and genetic distance using cranial measurements. Boyd found slight affinities between Middle Cumberland and Mouse Creek men, but not among women (Boyd and Boyd 1991). In a related study in 1985, Criss Helmkamp used mortuary and skeletal data from Late Woodland and Mississippian sites in the Upper Tennessee Valley to test biosocial markers and population interaction boundaries through time. His study distinguished social boundaries among Late Woodland groups of the Hamilton Complex, and it demonstrated a high level of regional integration among Mississippian communities. These higher levels of social interaction include a perceived increase in warfare during the Mississippian period. Maria Smith's (2003) study of interpersonal conflict in the Chickamauga Basin correlated skeletal trauma with low-intensity violence (ambushes and raiding) and possibly sanctioned violence against women.

PRESERVATION OF AND ACCESS TO THE NEW DEAL ARCHAEOLOGY COLLECTIONS

As can be inferred from the previous discussions, the archaeological collections from the New Deal projects include many types of objects and records. Some are suitable solely for basic archaeological research; others are of interest to a wider audience, including persons whose family members worked on the projects. Preservation of fragile objects, while providing appropriate access, is a challenge for all museums. A problem faced (and this is universal in museum collections) is the ongoing lack of adequate funding in accredited repositories for care of the New Deal-era collections. A recent *Science* article discussed curation difficulties at the McClung Museum and other institutions (Bawaya 2007). Although most New Deal-era collections are federally-owned or administered, and thus fall under federal curation regulations (36 CFR Part 79), federal agencies are reluctant to provide funds for their care, and many granting agencies will not award grants for "preservation, organization, or description of materials that are the responsibility of an agency of the federal government" (NEH Preservation and Access: Humanities Collections and Resources Grants Guidelines).

Nevertheless, museums are being creative about funding sources and are making it possible to negotiate the often conflicting goals of preservation and access so that some of these significant materials can be widely used for a variety of purposes and by diverse audiences. The online photo archive that we refer to throughout this article is one example of these projects. A complementary project was digitization of the original WPA excavation maps curated by the McClung Museum. These maps are extremely detailed drawings of all cultural features uncovered in the process of archaeological fieldwork. With help from the University Libraries and a large format scanner lent by TVA, some 500 New Deal-era maps now are scanned and archived. Although not online, digital copies of the maps are available for scholars to use, thus saving wear and tear on the original, now fragile, maps. A next step would be to make manipulation of the maps by researchers possible with Geographic Information System (GIS) software (O'Gorman 2007). But to digitize every posthole, pit, burial, stratigraphic level, and elevation point from every site map would require a new New Deal-sized workforce! Another project, funded by the Save America's Treasures grant program, is rehousing approximately 50,000 of the most fragile and temporally diagnostic artifacts in the WPA/TVA collections at the McClung to modern curatorial standards and creating a searchable, electronic database inventory of the collection. The new archival housing will help ensure that these materials will be available for generations to come, and the database will allow users to view photographs of objects and more easily find artifacts of interest.

THE LEGACY

The New Deal-era archaeology collections chronicle an important period in the histories of archaeology and of the United States, and they document the cultural heritage of the region's Native American peoples. That people of nearly every walk of life—coal miners, the rural poor, professionals, college students, politicians, agricultural workers, people of color, men, women, young people, the old and disabled—became involved in archaeology and in making these collections is an amazing story. The fact that the New Deal-era collections are of such high quality and are still adequate for answering provocative questions in archaeology and anthropology is a testament to the efforts of these people and their dedication and interest in this work. The New Deal collections represent a collective effort to learn about the past that will probably never be duplicated. The story of the making of these collections deserves to be better known and the wonderful materials they include to be more accessible to many people.

In the light of modern sensitivities about the injustices wrought by western cultures on American Indian cultures, some of the interests and methods of the Depression-era archaeology projects may now appear at odds with the values of the very cultures whose heritage the projects sought to preserve. We now know that the excavation of burial mounds and grave sites shows a lack of respect for many American Indian traditions, and the very curiosity that fueled the desire to learn about these ancient cultures can be attributed to a western intellectual tradition that may not be valued by others. These were not considerations of the New Deal archaeologists, nor were they considerations of the many laborers, the majority of whom were happy just to have a job. But, judging from the few available accounts, many of the workers were truly fascinated by the intellectual aspects of the archaeological research and the information it provided about ancient Native American life. As William Haag noted in 1985, it may well have been this appreciation of, and intellectual respect for, the past that led to the passage of modern historic preservation laws. These laws now require archaeological investigations before any federal land-altering projects. The fact that so many people had literally gotten their hands dirty on New Deal archaeology projects could only have helped with support for passage of such laws.

NOTES

1. Photographs for which the image numbers are provided in the text can be found by entering the DID number in one of the search boxes on the website's search page (do not include "DID"). This online archive was made possible by a grant from the Institute for Museum and Library Services (IMLS) to the UT Libraries and the McClung Museum. IMLS is not responsible for the content of the website or of this article.

2. Bauxar's original surname was Finkelstein.

WORKS CITED

Bawaya, Michael. 2007. "Curation in Crisis." *Science* 317:1025-1026.

Berryman, Hugh E. 1975. "A Multivariate Study of Three Prehistoric Tennessee Skeletal Populations: Mouse Creek, Dallas, and Middle Cumberland." Master's thesis, University of Tennessee.

Boyd, Donna C. 1984. "A Biological Investigation of Skeletal Remains from the Mouse Creek Phase and a Comparison with Two Late Mississippian Skeletal Populations from

Middle and East Tennessee." Master's thesis, University of Tennessee.

Boyd, Clifford C., and Donna C. Boyd. 1991. "A Multidimensional Investigation of Biocultural Relationships among Three Late Prehistoric Societies in Tennessee." *American Antiquity* 56: 75-88.

Braly, Bobby R., Shannon D. Koerner, Henri D. Grissino-Mayer, and Edward R. Cook. 2008. "Recent Dendroarchaeological Investigations at Late Period Sites in Eastern Tennessee." Paper presented at the 20th Annual Meeting, Current Research in Tennessee Archaeology, Nashville, Tennessee.

Claassen, Cheryl. 1999. Black and White Women at Irene Mound. In *Grit-Tempered: Early Women Archaeologists in the Southeastern United States*, edited by N. M. White, L. P. Sullivan, and R. Marrinan, 92-114. Florida Museum of Natural History, Ripley P. Bulletin Series. Gainesville: University Press of Florida.

Cole, Patricia E. 1975. "A Synthesis and Interpretation of the Hamilton Mortuary Pattern in East Tennessee." Master's thesis, University of Tennessee.

DeJarnette, David L., and Steve B. Wimberly. 1941. "The Bessemer Site: Excavation of the Three Mounds and Surrounding Village Areas Near Bessemer, Alabama." Museum Paper 17, Alabama Museum of Natural History. Tuscaloosa: University of Alabama.

Fagette, Paul. 1996. *Digging for Dollars: American Archaeology in the New Deal*. Albuquerque: University of New Mexico Press.

Gero, Joan. 1985. "Socio-politics of Archaeology and the Woman-at-Home Ideology." *American Antiquity* 50:342-350.

Haag, William G. 1985. "Federal Aid to Archaeology in the
        Southeast, 1933-1942." *American Antiquity* 50(2):272-280.

Harle, Michaelyn S. 2003. "A Bioarchaeological Analysis of Fains
        Island." Master's thesis, University of Tennessee.

Hatch, James W. 1974. "Social Dimension of Dallas Mortuary
        Practices." Master's thesis, Pennsylvania State University.

Hays-Gilpin, Kelly. 2000. "Feminist Scholarship in Archaeology."
        *Annals of the American Academy of Political and Social
        Science* 571: 89–106.

Hawley, Florence M. 1938. "Tree Ring Dating for Southeastern
        Mounds." In *An Archaeological Survey of the Norris Basin in
        Eastern Tennessee*, edited by W. S. Webb, 359-362. Bureau of
        American Ethnology. Bulletin 118. Smithsonian
        Institution. Washington, DC.: Government Printing Office.

Helmkamp, R. Criss. 1985. "Biosocial Organization and Change in
        East Tennessee Late Woodland and Mississippian."
        PhD diss., Purdue University.

Jennings, Jesse. 1994. *Accidental Archaeologist*. Salt Lake City:
        University of Utah Press.

Kentucky Heritage Council. 2002. *WPA Archaeology: Legacy of an
        Era*. Frankfort: Kentucky Archaeological Survey Video
        Series.

Kneberg, Madeline D. 1959. "Engraved Shell Gorgets and Their
        Associations." *Tennessee Archaeologist* 15(1):1-39.

Knight, Vernon James, Jr. 1993. "Obituary: David Lloyd DeJarnette
        1907-1991." *American Antiquity* 58(4):622-625.

Koerner, Shannon D., Henri D. Grissino-Mayer, and Lynne P.
        Sullivan. 2007. "Mississippian Site Occupational History:
        A Dendrochronological Approach." Paper presented at the

64th Annual Meeting. Southeastern Archaeological Conference, Knoxville, Tennessee.

Lewis, Thomas M. N., and Madeline D. Kneberg. 1941. *The Prehistory of the Chickamauga Basin in Tennessee: A Preview*. Tennessee Anthropology Papers No. 1. Division of Anthropology. Knoxville: University of Tennessee.

_____. 1946. *Hiwassee Island: An Archaeological Account of Four Tennessee Indian Peoples*. Knoxville: University of Tennessee Press.

Lewis, Thomas M. N. and Madeline Kneberg Lewis. 1961. *Eva: An Archaic Site*. Knoxville: University of Tennessee Press.

_____. 1995. *The Prehistory of the Chickamauga Basin in Tennessee*, compiled and edited by L. P. Sullivan. Knoxville: University of Tennessee Press.

Lyon, Edwin A. 1996. *A New Deal for Southeastern Archaeology*. Tuscaloosa: University of Alabama Press.

Milner, George R., and Virginia G. Smith. 1986. *New Deal Archaeology in Kentucky: Excavations, Collections, and Research*. Occasional Papers in Anthropology No. 5. Program for Cultural Resources Assessment. Lexington: University of Kentucky.

Nash, Charles H. 1968. "Residence Mounds: An Intermediate Middle-Mississippian Settlement Pattern." Master's Thesis, University of Mississippi.

Nash, Stephen Edward. 1999. *Time, Trees, and Prehistory: Tree-Ring Dating and The Development of North American Archaeology 1914-1950*. Salt Lake City: University of Utah Press.

Natonson, Nicholas, 1992. *The Black Image in the New Deal: The Politics of FSA Photography*. Knoxville: University of Tennessee Press.

O'Gorman, Jodie. 2007. "Rehabilitating Old Archaeology Collections with GIS. Collections." *A Journal for Museum and Archive Professionals* 3(1):75-101.

Peebles, Christopher S., Margaret J. Schoeninger, Vincas P. Steponaitis, and C. Margaret Scarry. 1981. "A Precious Bequest: Contemporary Research with the WPA-CCC Collections from Moundville, Alabama." *Annals of the New York Academy of Sciences* 376 (1):433-447.

Powell, Mary Lucas, Della Collins Cook, Georgieann Bogdan, Jane E. Buikstra, Mario M. Castro, Patrick D. Horne, David R. Hunt, Richard T. Koritzer, Sheila Ferraz Mendonca de Souza, Mary Kay Sandford, Laurie Saunders, Glaucia Aparecida Malerba Sene, Lynne Sullivan, John J. Swetnam. 2006. "Invisible Hands: Women in Bioarchaeology." In *A History of American Bioarchaeology: Peopling the Past*, edited by Jane E. Buikstra, 131-194. Burlington, MA: Elsevier Press.

Schroedl, Gerald F. 1978. "Excavations of the Leuty and McDonald Site Mounds in the Watts Bar Nuclear Plant Area." Report of Investigations No. 22. Department of Anthropology. Knoxville: University of Tennessee.

————. 1998. "Mississippian Towns in the Eastern Tennessee Valley." *In Mississippian Towns and Sacred Spaces*, edited by B. Lewis and C. Stout, 64-92. Tuscaloosa: University of Alabama Press.

Service, Elman R. 1962. *Primitive Social Organization*. New York: Random House.

Smith, Maria O. 2003. "Beyond Palisades: The Nature and Frequency of Late Prehistoric Deliberate Violent Trauma in the Chickamauga Reservoir of East Tennessee." *American Journal of Physical Anthropology* 121:303-318.

Smith, Monica. 2001. "The Archaeology of a 'Destroyed' Site: Surface Survey and Historical Documents at the CCC Camp, Bandelier National Monument, New Mexico." *Historical Archaeology* 35(2):31-40.

Sullivan, Lynne P. 1986. "*The Late Mississippian Village: Community and Society of the Mouse Creek Phase in Southeastern Tennessee.*" PhD diss., University of Wisconsin.

———. 1987. "The Mouse Creek Phase Household." *Southeastern Archaeology* 6(1):16-29.

———. 1989. "Cultural Change and Continuity in the Late Woodland and Early Mississippian Occupations of the Mouse Creeks Site." *Tennessee Anthropologist* 14:33-63.

———. 1995a. Foreword to *The Prehistory of the Chickamauga Basin in Tennessee,* compiled and edited by L. P. Sullivan. xv-xxviii. Knoxville: University of Tennessee Press.

———.1995b. "Mississippian Household and Community Organization in Eastern Tennessee." In *Mississippian Communities and Households*, edited by J. Daniel Rogers and Bruce D. Smith, 99-123. Tuscaloosa: University of Alabama Press.

———. 1999. "Madeline D. Kneberg Lewis: Leading Lady of Tennessee Archaeology." In *Grit-Tempered: Early Women Archaeologists in the Southeastern United States,* edited by N. M. White, L. P. Sullivan, and R. Marrinan, 57-91. Florida Museum of Natural History, Ripley P. Bulletin Series. Gainesville: University Press of Florida.

———. 2007a. "A WPA Déjà Vu on Mississippian Architecture." In *Architectural Variability in the Southeast: Comprehensive Case Studies of Mississippian Structures,* edited by Cameron H. Lacquement, 117-135. Tuscaloosa: University of Alabama Press.

————. 2007b. "Dating the Southeastern Ceremonial Complex in Eastern Tennessee." In *Southeastern Ceremonial Complex: Chronology, Iconography, and Style*, edited by A. King, 88-106. Tuscaloosa: University of Alabama Press.

————, and Michaelyn S. Harle. 2010. "Mortuary Practices and Cultural Identity at the Turn of the Sixteenth Century in Eastern Tennessee." In *Mississippian Mortuary Practices: Beyond Hierarchy and the Representationist Perspective*, edited by L.P. Sullivan and R. C. Mainfort, Jr., 234-249. Gainesville: University Press of Florida Press.

Taylor, Nick. 2008. *American-Made: The Enduring Legacy of the WPA: When FDR Put the Nation to Work*. New York: Bantam Books.

Vogel, Juliette R. 2007. "Mound versus Village: A Biocultural Investigation of Status and Health at the Cox Site." Master's thesis, University of Tennessee.

Walker, Jesse. 1994. "Haag, William, collection #4700.0453, Louisiana and Lower Mississippi Valley Collections." Hill Memorial Library. Baton Rouge: Louisiana State University.

Webb, William S. 1938. *An Archaeological Survey of the Norris Basin in Eastern Tennessee*. Bureau of American Ethnology Bulletin 118. Smithsonian Institution. Washington, DC: Government Printing Office.

————. 1939. *An Archaeological Survey of Wheeler Basin on the Tennessee River in Northern Alabama*. Bureau of American Ethnology Bulletin 122, Smithsonian Institution. Washington, DC: Government Printing Office.

————. 1940. "Cypress Creek Villages, Sites 11 and 12, McLean County, Kentucky." *Reports in Anthropology* 4(2). Lexington: University of Kentucky.

_____. 1947a. "Archaic Sites in McLean County, Kentucky." *Reports in Anthropology in Anthropology* 7(1). Lexington: University of Kentucky.

_____. 1947b. "The Fisher Site, Fayette County, Kentucky." *Reports in Anthropology and Archaeology* 7(2). Lexington: University of Kentucky.

_____. 1948a. *The Whitesburg Bridge Site (Ma10). Geological Survey of Alabama.* Tuscaloosa: University of Alabama Press.

_____. 1948b. "Flint River Site (Ma48), Madison County, Alabama." Museum Paper No. 23, Alabama Museum of Natural History. Tuscaloosa: University of Alabama.

Webb, William S., and David L. DeJarnette. 1942. *An Archeological Survey of Pickwick Basin in the Adjacent Portions of the States of Alabama, Mississippi and Tennessee.* Bureau of American Ethnology Bulletin 129, Smithsonian Institution. Washington, DC: Government Printing Office.

Webb, William S., and William G. Haag. 1939. "The Chiggerville Site, Site 1, Ohio County, Kentucky." *Reports in Anthropology* 4(1). Lexington: University of Kentucky.

Webb, William S., and Charles G. Wilder. 1951. *An Archaeological Survey of Guntersville Basin on the Tennessee River in Northern Alabama.* Lexington: University of Kentucky Press.

Whalen Gail. 2008. *Elusive Women of Irene: The WPA Excavation of Irene Mound.* http://www.sip.armstrong.edu/Irene/essay.html.

White, Nancy M. 1999. "Women in Southeastern U.S. Archaeology." In *Grit-Tempered: Early Women Archaeologists in the Southeastern United States,* edited by Nancy M. White, Lynne P. Sullivan, and Rochelle Marrinan, 92-114. Florida

Museum of Natural History, Ripley P. Bulletin Series. Gainesville: University Press of Florida.

Willey, Gordon R., and Jeremy A. Sabloff, 1974. *A History of American Archaeology*. San Francisco: W. H. Freeman.

Memory Within a University Landscape

Laura J. Galke, George Washington Foundation
Bernard K. Means, Virginia Commonwealth University

INTRODUCTION

Anthropologists have long recognized that significant aspects of en-culturation and how people define their place in the world rest on the interaction between individuals and their constructed landscapes. People learn their place in society—and the places of others—from elements of the built environment and from the world of objects that surrounds them (Bourdieu 1977; Rapoport 1990). Essentially, individuals and groups base actions on how they interact with inhab-ited space, with the objects in that space, and with each other within that space (Blanton 1994, 19). Spatial structure "reinforces to some degree a customary pattern of interaction among its occupants and this instills and reinforces a cognitive model" of the social order (Blanton 1994, 19). In addition, dominant groups—economic, social, political—may deliberately create or destroy elements of a constructed landscape in order to provide an ideological justification for their privileged positions (Shackel 2008).

Washington and Lee University is a modern institution that traces its history back to a small, mid-eighteenth-century academy. Memories created from this extensive history have shaped the con-temporary university landscape in ways that have both reflected and influenced ideology through time. Choices made regarding what pasts are commemorated and what pasts are de-emphasized or excluded are part of the process of creating heritage. Using historical documents, archaeological discoveries, and the university's cultural landscape, this paper illustrates how the contemporary Washington and Lee University campus communicates, commemorates, and illustrates its past to the community. Archaeological excavations performed on the eighteenth- and nineteenth-century Washington and Lee University campuses, respectively, have provided students with the opportunity to evaluate popular histories of their school (Galke 2005a,b, 2006a,b,c, 2007; Greco 2007; Jackson 2006, 2007a,b,c; McDaniel et al. 1994).

ARCHAEOLOGY AND MEMORY

Groups and individual persons pursue different strategies to manipulate, modify, and even create memories of past events and use these memories to justify the social order of which they are a part. These historical memories may glamorize or sanitize an individual, group, or event (Shackel 2008, 10). Official public memories of places are designed to glamorize the past of dominant social groups, often at the expense of subaltern groups. Shackel asserts that "understanding how and why some groups tend to remember a particular past, while others forget or ignore a past, is an important issue for critically evaluating and understanding the development and meaning of the past" (2008, 10). Archaeological efforts can be brought to bear on the study of official public memories because these memories are often directly tied to tangible features on the landscape, including statues, cemeteries, and buildings. Usually invisible features of the landscape, such as buried archaeological deposits, can bear witness to a dominant group's efforts to sanitize historical memories associated with events that challenge official orthodoxy, have associations with subaltern groups, or both.

One major strategy for generating historical memories in the present is to create an exclusionary past that is more about forgetting persons or events than remembering something specific about the past. This is evident in cases related to race and genocide (Shackel 2008, 10). For example, the African American town of Rosewood, Florida, was destroyed in an orgy of racial violence in 1923 (Davidson and González-Tennant 2008). "Archaeology is seen as a way to commemorate and remember the place and event, while the white community is thwarting any efforts to study and remember the place" (Shackel 2008, 11). Another example is provided by archaeological excavations at the Alamo. These excavations recovered materials from the infamous 1836 battle, and in addition they have revealed a rich record reflecting the eighteenth-century Spanish mission period of the Alamo. Today, over half of the population of San Antonio is of Latino descent, and they are eager to have a more positive role in the presented history of the Alamo. This shift in emphasis is being resisted by some, including the Daughters of the Republic of Texas, who risk losing their preeminent status in a more inclusive interpretive environment (Flores 2002; Thomas 2002, 135).

Another strategy for generating historical memories is to commemorate a patriotic figure or event, often supported with sanctioned observations (Shackel 2008, 11). The Lost Cause of the Confederacy is celebrated throughout the South (Wilson 1980), and several prominent historical figures are honored in Lexington, Virginia, where Washington and Lee University is located. Every January on the Friday before the observance of Martin Luther King Jr. Day, Lee-Jackson Day celebrates two prominent figures associated with the Lost Cause. A parade begins at Stonewall Jackson's grave in his eponymous cemetery and proceeds down Main Street to Robert E. Lee's resting place in the aptly named Lee Chapel, located on the campus of Washington and Lee. Men and boys in grey Confederate uniforms and women in hoop skirts participate in this parade and use these two locations to reinforce a popular collective memory of a romanticized past. We will return to the topic of Lee Chapel shortly. Historical memories can also be generated through an emphasis on heritage, "whereby current social and political circumstances are seen to have a long tradition… Heritage connotes integrity, authenticity, venerability, and stability" (Shackel 2008, 11).

WASHINGTON AND LEE UNIVERSITY: A BRIEF INTRODUCTION

Here, we want to take a moment and talk specifically about Washington and Lee University, before we consider how the constructed landscape of the campus—and its buried archaeological resources—are used to create and accord legitimacy to established narratives. Archaeology can play a significant role in stimulating critical consideration of these popular historical memories. Washington and Lee University is a small, private liberal arts institution located in Lexington, Virginia, one which takes great pride in its history and traditions. The school traces its roots back to an academy that was established in 1749. It possesses a number of historical buildings that are listed on the National Register. The National Register of Historic Places lists physical locations of national significance throughout the United States based upon four criteria. The list includes sites:

> A. That are associated with events that have made a significant contribution to the broad patterns of our history; or

> B. That are associated with the lives of persons significant in our past; or

C. That embody the distinctive characteristics of a type, period, or method of construction, or that represent the work of a master, or that possess high artistic values, or that represent a significant and distinguishable entity whose components may lack individual distinction; or

D. That have yielded or may be likely to yield, information important in prehistory or history (National Park Service 2008).

Individual buildings on the campus that are listed on the Register include the remains of the late eighteenth-century Washington Academy academic building, Lee Chapel, and Washington Hall, among others (Galke 2007). The standing ruins of the Academy structure, built in 1793, are known to the campus community as "The Ruins" and remain preserved as part of the modern campus. The Ruins form a backdrop to many campus events and activities. This small, private university has recently taken formal steps to expand the preservation of its historic campus landscape and architectural treasures, including the creation of a campus preservation plan (Carras and Gilliam 2004). In addition, a decades-long archaeology program at Washington and Lee University has investigated portions of its eighteenth-century campus and its nineteenth-century dormitories, which survive archaeologically (Galke 2005a,b, 2006c, 2007; Jackson 2007a,b,c).

HISTORICAL FIGURES AND THE MAKING OF THE UNIVERSITY

Not surprisingly, a significant component of the popular historical memory of Washington and Lee University revolves around the school's two namesakes (Jackson 2007a,b,c). George Washington's name first became attached to the university at the close of the eighteenth century, thanks to his gift of James River canal stock. Washington's donation proved critical to the survival of this school, which was teetering on the brink of insolvency in the years surrounding the American Revolution (Crenshaw 1969). Every Washington and Lee University student today has this event integrated into their memory of the University because they learn as freshmen that a portion of their own tuition is paid for through Washington's bequest (Scott 1997). In addition to Washington's name displayed throughout the university, including on merchandise, a statue of Washington graces the top of the central building of the Colonnade (discussed below) that was re-named in Washington's honor.

While Washington's statue atop Washington Hall forms a visible anchor for the creation of sanctioned historical memories, George Washington's presence is overshadowed by that of Robert E. Lee on the constructed landscape of the campus. Robert E. Lee was president of Washington College for five years following the American Civil War. His name was appended to that of Washington to form the school's current name upon Lee's death in 1870 (Crenshaw 1969). Lee's connection to Washington and Lee University was obviously more immediate than Washington's was. He left behind many tangible features on the main campus landscape that assist in creating historical memories of his presence on the campus. Lee lived in the president's house, now named for him; and the University's Chapel, built at his urging, is also named after Lee. The Chapel is a central component of today's campus landscape, facing the University's hallowed Colonnade. Enhancing the generation of historical memory focused on Lee is the fact that Lee and his family are interred together in a crypt constructed on the back of Lee Chapel. Members of Lee's family, including his father, Revolutionary war hero Henry "Light

Horse Harry" Lee, were disinterred from their original resting places and moved to the Lee family crypt.

Lee Chapel also houses a museum in its basement offering an exhibition of Lee's office, ostensibly as he left it upon his death (although surviving photographs indicate that it was straightened up a bit post mortem). The Chapel's recently launched exhibition acknowledges this fact. Lee's horse Traveller has a privileged burial site just outside the Lee family crypt, as well as a brochure and a student bus service named in his honor.

William Graham is a recognized historical figure on the campus as well, though in a much more subdued fashion. Graham was rector of the institution in the eighteenth century and was actually responsible for moving the school to the outskirts of Lexington in 1780 (McDaniel et al. 1994, 39). Yet Graham's eighteenth-century contributions to Washington and Lee University are literally buried in the shadow of Lee Chapel. Here, William Graham's remains rest in a less prominent place than the remains of Lee's horse—despite the extreme efforts the University exerted to have Graham's remains disinterred from his original burial site in Richmond and moved to their current location.

It is difficult to find a historical memory of Washington and Lee University that does not involve Lee. Lee eclipses Washington in the formation of historical memories on campus, sometimes in subtle ways. The Morris House is used for guests of the University like alumni and members of the Board, and it has rooms named after Lee and Washington. Washington's room is modest and contains small portraits of the country's first President. The Lee suite contains two, substantially nicer, rooms, one of which contains a life-sized image of the former Confederate general. In a recent class on historical archaeology taught by the senior author, in which students were introduced to the ideas of critical archaeology and the suppression of subaltern groups in popular history, one group who created a presentation on the racial dimensions of historical commemoration on campus nevertheless ended that presentation with a picture of Lee and Traveller, with the former resplendent in his Confederate uniform.

THE WASHINGTON AND LEE UNIVERSITY COLONNADE AND THE MODERN CAMPUS IDENTITY

Several aspects of campus history are not highlighted by the school today, and therefore are not part of the historical memory that is commemorated by the community through their interaction with the constructed landscape and, significantly, its virtual extension on the Internet. The historic Colonnade represents the core of the Washington and Lee University campus today. Beginning in 2004, the University used a J. Paul Getty Trust Campus Heritage Grant to create a comprehensive Historic Preservation Master Plan. The grant also funded the development and implementation of courses designed to provide students with practical experience in heritage management using the campus history and cultural resources (Carras and Gilliam 2004, 7-8, 25).

Most of the Colonnade buildings lack modern conveniences such as central air conditioning, fire alarm systems, handicapped access, and elevators (Carras and Gilliam 2004, 3). As a result of substantial interior alterations to all of these structures during the mid-1930s (Carras and Gilliam 2004, 3), the interiors of these impressive structures possess no integrity related to their original, nineteenth-century construction (John Milner Associates, Inc. 2005, 5-2). The absence of historic integrity is considered unimportant in terms of creating historical memories today. More important is that the exterior of the Colonnade buildings *appear* to represent an integrated entity.

The Colonnade certainly has an imposing physical presence, given its prominent location on a ridge overlooking the surrounding town. The Colonnade's stately appearance projects to the University and its extended community an historical memory that includes a heritage focused on the education of young minds, overwhelmingly white and male until the mid-twentieth century. However, the Colonnade is actually a culmination of a dynamic architectural history. The two structures that were originally built by the then College on this ridge in 1804 are long gone, but all of the buildings that exist on the Colonnade today are positioned relative to these demolished structures. In 1824, Washington Hall was the third building constructed by the College on this ridge; popular histories privilege this structure, and most people believe that it is the Colonnade's first structure, when it is simply the oldest *extant* building.

The remainder of the nineteenth century and the first part of the twentieth century saw a number of Colonnade buildings demolished, new ones built in their places, and the replacement of a building that was destroyed by fire. Architectural flourishes that provide the Colonnade with its uniform appearance and sense of historic precedence—notably, the columns—were added to some buildings long after they were built. Other visual cues that enhance the integrity and uniformity of the Colonnade are relatively recent; faculty members in the history department recall the diversity in brick hues that reflected the Colonnade's construction history. The generous application of unifying brick-red paint in the mid-twentieth century, however, camouflages the visible historical evidence of change. This illusion of a static history recently prompted some in the campus community to question the need for archaeology in this venerated space.

Thus, the Colonnade projects antiquity, authority, and authentic heritage for the University, which is integrated in efforts to create an official historical memory. What this official historical memory does not reflect, in addition to the Colonnade's dynamic architectural history, is that a major source of funds used to support a particularly active building episode in the 1840s was the sale of enslaved Americans (Jackson 2007b). In fact, unlike the efforts of UNC Chapel Hill (Ballinger et al. 2008), which has recognized that enslaved Americans contributed to their institution and helped to build its structures, Washington and Lee University has been reluctant to acknowledge its ownership and sale of enslaved Americans. Rather, in an attempt to counter a virtually monolithic historical memory focused on Robert E. Lee, the University has begun to highlight the achievements of John Chavis, a free African American who attended Washington Hall Academy at the close of the eighteenth century (Jackson 2007b). While this effort is indeed laudable, John Chavis was atypical of the African American experience at this institution: no other student of African descent would be admitted to Washington and Lee University until over 160 years later. In addition, there is no commemoration of Chavis at the site of the late-eighteenth-century Washington Academy Ruins, where he attended classes. However, there is signage at the Ruins recognizing the contributions of a recent member of the coaching staff.

There is no clear motivation to create an historical memory that highlights the entire Black American heritage at Washington and Lee University. This is partly because the local African American community is numerically small and politically marginalized relative to the town's white population. Furthermore, Washington and Lee University's student body, although slowly becoming more diversified—diversification is a major emphasis of the current University administration—is predominantly still white and southern.

Another aspect of historical memory that can be examined at Washington and Lee University is evolving ideas concerning student and faculty responsibilities at Washington Academy between the years 1793-1891. A clear transition from a cloistered eighteenth-century academy to a more modern student body is evident in the constructed landscape, architecture, and artifacts recovered from the eighteenth- and nineteenth-century campuses. Nineteenth-century students rejected the traditional seclusion, thorough scheduling, and conspicuous surveillance that characterized the eighteenth-century academy. Students came to expect increased privacy and expanded interaction with the nearby townspeople, even as the College experimented with more subtle methods of supervision (Galke 2005a,b, 2006c).

ARCHAEOLOGICAL EXCAVATIONS AT WASHINGTON AND LEE

Situated on the northern portion of the main campus today, the Ruins are the most visible evidence of the historic Washington Academy campus, precursor to today's Washington and Lee University. The eighteenth-century campus was located outside the town limits of Lexington in a deliberate attempt to preserve a secluded academic community focused on study and prayer. Between 1974 and 1979, the Department of Sociology and Anthropology conducted extensive archaeological investigations on this northern portion of the contemporary campus (McDaniel et al. 1994). Student excavations recovered several categories of artifacts that indicated that the school's official rules were breached despite the academy's secluded location (McDaniel et al. 1994, 141-142). The results from these investigations are regularly featured in the curriculum as a case study in archaeology for "Introduction to Anthropology" courses, enabling students to develop an expanded historical memory of their campus history.

After fire destroyed the stone academy building in 1803, the institution reluctantly acquiesced to community pressure to move within

the town limits. Once in the city limits, Washington Academy built
Union Hall and Graham Hall, structures which shared the aesthetics
and functionality of the eighteenth-century academy building, serv-
ing both as classroom space and as student living quarters. However,
unlike the eighteenth-century academy building, the administration
situated the student quarters on the first floor rather than the upper
floors, ensuring that faculty might better observe student behavior
outside the classroom. Rules published in 1839 allowed faculty to enter student rooms at any time of the day or night. Both Union Hall
and Graham Hall were demolished in 1835 and each was replaced
by a single-story brick dormitory. These dormitories were designed
to facilitate scrutiny and control over students. No windows were
allowed on the front façade, which faced the town. There were neither connecting doorways nor hallways in the interior. In the next
six years, faculty housing was built adjacent to the dormitory, ex-
plicitly to facilitate surveillance of students. Any question over how
the students felt about these dormitories is evident in their monikers
for these structures: they were colloquially referred to as "Hell" and
"Purgatory" (Galke 2005a,b, 2006b,c).

Distinct differences in the nature of artifacts recovered from
the eighteenth-century "outside town limits" campus and the nineteenth-century "in-town" campus reflect a dramatic change in student activities. The eighteenth-century campus, excavated during
the 1970s, contained marbles, smoking pipes, and evidence of games
that used dominoes and dice. In stark contrast, recent excavations
on the 19th-century campus found absolutely no evidence for any of
these activities (Galke 2005b, 2006c). Either increased scrutiny pre-
vented students from engaging in them, or the proximity of town
provided a crucial alternative for these recreational behaviors. In
addition, the recovery of a pointer, possibly used for physical pun-

ishment, suggests physical discipline may have been a part of this antebellum environment.

Multiple lines of evidence demonstrate that Washington Academy used the built environment to help monitor student behavior. Contrary to the institution's serious concerns about the effect that moving the school within the town limits would have upon student behavior, the nineteenth-century campus assemblage reflected fewer extra-curricular activities. The apparent absence of recreational artifacts seems to be the result of a constructed landscape that promoted the surveillance of students and, by the proximity of the town itself, served as an alternative venue for forbidden or discouraged activities.

The recent excavations on the nineteenth-century campus were located on the University's Colonnade. Visitors were frequent and included students, faculty, staff, and alumni. During the course of the investigation, we engaged the public in the creation of historic memories through signage, a site brochure, and a webpage, designed by Bernard K. Means, that is currently linked to the department's webpage. Prospective students and their parents dropped by, or viewed the site as part of formal campus tours. In addition, visitors from the general public were also welcome recipients of our interpretations and investigations. The site was located within an easy walk of the nearby town and campus attractions such as Lee Chapel, where the Lee family remains at rest. Interaction with the public was unavoidable, and the signage and brochures made contacts with them easier and more informative.

Because this particular site yielded material culture related to the students who attended this institution throughout the nineteenth century, field school students—all attending Washington and Lee University—were easily engaged in the project's discoveries. Historic issues regarding student behavior, obtrusive faculty surveillance, and the relationship between the campus and local community were significant issues in the past and continue to influence Washington and Lee University students and the surrounding community today. Because students were investigating the lives of their predecessors, the history of their own university, and issues that had historical precedents, their interest in the work seemed especially enthusiastic. Students had little difficulty relating how the data that they were collecting related to their lives today, and how the material culture reflected issues that had been part of the relationship between university administration and students for generations at our institution. Students made the connection between the artifacts that they were finding and the contemporary society of which they are members. We provided students with the opportunity to critically evaluate popular campus histories. Students participated in the creation of their own revised historical memories that expanded on the more sanitized official version presented by the industry on campus tours and on the school's webpage.

CONCLUSIONS

One insidious influence of the cultural landscape is that it appears timeless. Therein exists its authority and, for some, its potential for manipulation. Yet the stories that we promote using this landscape are dynamic. Through awareness of the heritage-making process and its uses, we can recognize the ideology behind popular histories and expand our current commemorations of the past to be more inclusive, more complex, and richer.

WORKS CITED

Ballinger, Susan, Bari Helms, and Janis Holder. 2008. Slavery and
    the Making of the University. Unpublished Manuscript held

at University of North Carolina at Chapel Hill. http://www.
    lib.unc.edu/mss/ exhibits/ slavery/index.html.

Blanton, Richard. 1994. *Houses and Household: A Comparative
    Study*. New York: Plenum Press.

Bourdieu, Pierre. 1977. *Outline of a Theory of Practice*. Cambridge:
    Cambridge University Press.

Carras, George P., and Catharine M. Gilliam. 2004. Application to
    the Getty Grant Program Campus Heritage Grants.
    Prepared by Washington and Lee University. Submitted to
    the Getty Grant Program, Los Angeles, California.

Crenshaw, Ollinger. 1969. *General Lee's College: The Rise and Growth
    of Washington and Lee University*. New York: Random House.

Davidson, James M., and Edward González-Tennant. 2008. "A
    Potential Archaeology of Rosewood, Florida: The Process of
    Remembering a Community and a Tragedy." *The SAA
    Archaeological Record* 8(1):13-16.

Flores, Richard B. 2002. *Remembering the Alamo: Memory,
    Modernity, and the Master Symbol*. Austin: University of
    Texas Press.

Galke, Laura J. 2005a. "Student Life and Discipline at Washington
    Academy." Paper presented at the Eastern States
    Archaeological Federation, Williamsburg, Virginia.
    Manuscript on file at the Anthropology Laboratory.
    Lexington, VA: Washington and Lee University.

———. 2005b. "Archaeology on Washington and Lee University's
    Colonnade." Paper presented at the Middle Atlantic
    Archaeology Conference, Rehoboth Beach, Delaware.
    Manuscript on file at the Anthropology Laboratory.
    Lexington, VA: Washington and Lee University.

————. 2006a. Summary Report of ANTH 290 Historical Landscapes and ANTH 403 Independent Study on Liberty Hall Academy. Manuscript on file at the Anthropology Laboratory. Lexington, VA: Washington and Lee University.

————. 2006b. Report on Results of the 2005 Archaeological Test Excavations of the Antebellum Structures Beside Newcomb Hall 44RB489B. Manuscript on file at the Anthropology Laboratory. Lexington, VA: Washington and Lee University.

————. 2006c. "Constructing Discipline, Deconstructing Ideology: The Archaeology and History of Washington and Lee's Antebellum Dormitories." *Journal of Middle Atlantic Archaeology* 22:19-29.

————. 2007. "Scholarship in Ruins: Archaeology and Preservation in an Academic Environment." *Journal of Middle Atlantic Archaeology* 23:85-95.

————. 2010. "Post-Revolutionary Degeneracy: Washington and Lee University's Landscape of Control." In *Beneath the Ivory Tower: The Archaeology of Academia*, edited by Russell K. Skowronek and Kenneth E. Lewis, 164-181. Gainesville: University Press of Florida.

Greco, Edmund. 2007. "Little Town, Big Sins." Paper presented at the Annual Meeting of the Archeological Society of Virginia, Williamsburg, Virginia.

Jackson, Abbie. 2006. History and Archaeology of Washington and Lee University: An Intersite Analysis and Exhibit Design for the Anthropology Lab. Robert E. Lee Grant final Report. Manuscript on file at the Anthropology Laboratory. Lexington, VA: Washington and Lee University.

————. 2007a. "Representation Issues and the History and Archaeology of Washington and Lee University." *Journal of Middle Atlantic Archaeology* 23:97-103.

————. 2007b. "Representation Issues and the History and Archaeology of Washington and Lee University." Honors thesis, Washington and Lee University.

————. 2007c. "A Second Look at Representation Issues at Washington and Lee University." Paper presented at the Annual Meeting of the Archeological Society of Virginia, Williamsburg, Virginia.

John Milner Associates, Inc. 2005. Preservation Master Plan for Washington and Lee University, Lexington, Virginia. Manuscript prepared for Washington and Lee University. West Chester, PA: John Milner Associates, Inc.

Little, Barbara. 2007. *Historical Archaeology: Why the Past Matters*. Walnut Creek, CA: Left Coast Press.

McDaniel, John M., Kurt C. Russ, and Parker B. Potter. 1994. "An Archaeological and Historical Assessment of the Liberty Hall Academy Complex 1782-1803." In *The James G. Leyburn Papers in Anthropology*, vol. II. Lexington, VA: Liberty Hall Press.

National Park Service. 2008. Listing a Property: Some Frequently Asked Questions. http://www.nps.gov/history/nr/listing.htm.

Rapoport, Amos, 1990. *The Meaning of the Built Environment: A Nonverbal Communication Approach*. Tucson: University of Arizona Press.

Scott, Glenn Allen, 1997. "Washington's Gift to a Small Lexington School Keeps on Giving. WandL Marks its 250th Anniversary In 1999. That it Survives to a Ripe Age Is Due in No Small Measure To Washington's Generosity." *The Virginian-Pilot*, July 2. http://scholar.lib.vt.edu/VA-news/VA-Pilot/issues/1997/vp970702/07020004.htm.

Shackel, Paul. 2008. "Memory Studies in Historical Archaeology." *The SAA Archaeological Record* 8(1):10-12.

Thomas, David Hurst. 2002. "Roadside Ruins: Does America Still Need Archaeology Museums?" In *Public Benefits of Archaeology*, edited by Barbara J. Little, 130-145. Tallahassee: University Press of Florida.

Waldrop, Preston. n.d. Deed Trace At Liberty Hall Farm and Land. Unpublished manuscript on file at the Anthropology Laboratory. Lexington, VA: Washington and Lee University.

Wilson, Charles Reagan, 1980. "The Religion of the Lost Cause: Ritual and Organization of the Southern Civil Religion, 1865-1920." *The Journal of Southern History* 46(2):219-238.

The Jamestown Commemoration of 2007: Remembering Our Diversity in the Past and Present

Vincent H. Melomo, Peace College

> "The Far East has its Mecca, Palestine its Jerusalem, France its Lourdes, and Italy its Loretto, but America's only shrines are her altars of patriotism—the first and most potent being Jamestown; the sire of Virginia, and Virginia the mother of this great Republic..."
> —From a 1907 Virginia guidebook (APVA 2000)

INTRODUCTION

The 400th anniversary of the initial settlement of Jamestown in 1607 provided an important opportunity for us to reflect on the recent public commemoration of this early English presence in the land that became the United States. While much has been written in both an academic and popular vein about Jamestown in the years surrounding the 400th anniversary (Horn 2006, Kelso 2006, Kupperman 2007, Rountree 2006, Woolley 2008), little has been written discussing the significance of the commemoration itself as a cultural phenomenon. To this end, this paper focuses on the more public aspects of the Jamestown Commemoration of 2007; and, in particular, it explores the significance of this commemoration in relation to our past and present diversity, a diversity that includes—and exceeds—red, black, and white.[1]

Before addressing the Jamestown Commemoration directly, I want to comment on my own background as it contributes to an understanding of my approach. Unlike those usually offering comment on Jamestown, I am neither an archaeologist of contact nor an historian of colonial America. Rather, I am a cultural anthropologist with an interest in these areas. I have a somewhat peculiar academic history in that my master's research was on the archaeology and history of the contact period (Melomo 1994), and my doctoral research was on contemporary issues of race and ethnicity (Melomo 2003). The focus of my research has been primarily on the original "Indians"; that is, South Asian Americans, who are mostly relatively recent immigrants to this country. However, having a background in archaeology and teaching at a small liberal arts college, I have offered an introduction to archaeology course for most of the past ten years that has included an annual pilgrimage to the Jamestown site. Through these visits, through further reflection, and through some further research, I have sought to make some sense of Jamestown in relation to our history and our contemporary context. This paper is thus an attempt to reconcile my peculiar history and interests, as well as the peculiarity of the stories that we tell about our past and our present, and thus ourselves.

When I first began reflecting on the topic of Jamestown, I was struck by the oddity of a celebration of Englishness at this moment in the history of the U.S. and of the South in particular. We live in a time when diversity is increasingly acknowledged and celebrated; when diversity in terms of ethnicity, language, and religion is on the rise; and when global connections are expanding and increasingly considered important. However, this is also a time when efforts to embrace that diversity are still being strongly contested, and global interactions are also often seen as threatening, particularly by anti-immigrant nativists and Christian nationalists. Given these contradictory realities, I felt it important to explore the significance of a Jamestown Commemoration in this context. To do so, in this paper

I first argue that Jamestown is most significantly a national symbol; then, I consider some specific meanings given to Jamestown as a national symbol; and then, I explore the relevance of Jamestown to our contemporary diversity. In addressing the latter point, I discuss how the complex context of Jamestown in the 17th century provides some interesting correlations with our current situation, offering us an important opportunity for constructing a national creation story that speaks more to our current diversity, albeit perhaps in complicated ways.

JAMESTOWN AS NATIONAL SYMBOL

Jamestown is a place, a geography, a landscape where people acted and made history. However, Jamestown's significance for my discussion is less in terms of the particulars of actors and events in this history and more in terms of how we remember their broader significance—or do not remember them—and how we reconstitute them in relation to the present. In this sense, Jamestown is perhaps best understood as a symbol of that imagined community of a nation (Anderson 1991[1983]). The commemoration of Jamestown every fifty years can be seen as the ritual process that reinforces the power of that symbol and reconfigures its meaning. Jamestown Commemorations can thus be understood as a kind of invented tradition, one that is part of the process of defining who we are as a people (Hobsbawm 1983). This is ultimately what makes Jamestown so interesting, and so important.

Jamestown has for over a hundred years been celebrated as "the birthplace of our nation." Tracing the origins of any identity, value, or behavior is always a terribly complicated affair. Trying to identify where "America" began or where "democracy" originated is a little like paleoanthropologists and archaeologists trying to trace when we became human; such research is always interesting, but hardly ever definitive. It is clear that the political entity known as the United States that now spreads from the Atlantic into the Pacific is tied to the history at Jamestown, perhaps most specifically in the fact that I am speaking to you in English right now. However, it is also important to note that the settlers at Jamestown could not possibly have imagined the U.S. in its current manifestation and certainly had virtually no notion of an American identity, or of a United States. While Jamestown was certainly of great historical significance to the U.S., I suggest that we could have a strikingly similar, complicated state, varied population, and national identity, with or without Jamestown.

Nevertheless, in 2007, Jamestown was commemorated in a way that virtually no other place in our country has been so far. Jamestown was celebrated as *the* national symbol, *the* origin story, *the* creation myth of our state. Recognized widely as the birthplace of our nation, it was celebrated as the place where democracy, liberty, diversity, freedom of religion, free enterprise, a spirit of exploration, hard work, determination, the rule of law, private property, and virtually all that is thought good in America had originated. As Kupperman states in *The Jamestown Project*, however, when looked at closely, Jamestown can also be seen as "the creation story from hell," the place where Native Americans were slaughtered, Africans enslaved, people starved, industries failed, and martial law sometimes prevailed (Kupperman 2007, 1). The ugly warts of the Jamestown project, though better acknowledged in the 2007 Commemoration than in the past, have not been enough to unsettle Jamestown's place in our creation myth.

Apart from being recognized as the birthplace of America, Jamestown is also most often, and more definitively, recognized as the earliest permanent English settlement in what became the U.S. It is important to consider then that Jamestown could have been celebrated not as America's story writ large, but as the story of a specific people, the English in the Americas. The fact that it was not commemorated in this way only helps to reinforce the place of the English in U.S. history and culture. What is implicit in the ritual focus on Jamestown as the birthplace of America is that the Anglo tradition and identity is the American one. Understood through Barthes' (1972) concept of exnomination, the ideology of English (or perhaps White) superiority in America is thus taken for granted by going unnamed. However, since the Jamestown Commemoration was not just a celebration of Englishness, but rather a celebration of some non-ethnically specific Americanness, then the question remains, what is being celebrated? What do we commemorate about being "American" following from this colonial settlement?

JAMESTOWN AND DEMOCRACY

Recent writings and commentary on Jamestown most typically refer to democracy as the key virtue inherited from the early settlers at the site. Portrayed sometimes as a veritable Athens of the New World, Jamestown is said to be the location of the first representative assembly some twelve years into its troubled existence. Of course, one need only give that early history just a glance to come to the conclusion that Jamestown was not a democracy that most of us would recognize, support, and promote today. If we see democracy as a government of, by, and for the people, then Jamestown is left badly wanting. My point here is to suggest that the Jamestown Commemoration was as much, or more, a celebration of the idea of democracy, and of the idea of America, as it was a celebration of an historic reality; and thus we should understand that Jamestown's significance today is perhaps really more symbolic than historical.

Perhaps one of the most interesting, and potentially important, appropriations of Jamestown as a national symbol was by the current head of the executive of these United States, George Bush. President Bush delivered an address at Jamestown as part of America's Anniversary Weekend (Bush 2007). Of course the very presence of the President at the commemoration is part of the process through which Jamestown is affirmed as a national symbol. In his address at the commemoration ceremony, Bush essentially offered a story of America as an ever-expanding democracy, politically, and geographically. In his remarks he linked the present and the past by referring to the settlers at Jamestown along with the countries of Afghanistan and Iraq. A myth about the past was used to reinforce a myth about our present. In his speech he called upon us to see the settlement of Jamestown as an important early effort to spread democracy. Of course this is the same argument Bush makes for supporting the military invasions of Iraq and Afghanistan; that is, to spread democracy. Bush also linked the past and the present by suggesting that commemorating our ties to the English at Jamestown makes sense today because the English and the U.S. are brothers in arms in the continuing fight to spread democracy around the world.

Through Bush's commemoration address we see most clearly the elevation of Jamestown to a national symbol, and a symbol of democracy; and we see the clear association of the English with this symbol, in both the present and the past. Bush's remarks at the commemoration could, however, otherwise be seen as inclusive, clearly acknowledging the place that Native Americans and African Americans had in his American story. As I now discuss, however, some American groups felt excluded by Bush's inclusiveness, and other American groups simply were not part of the commemoration at all.

JAMESTOWN AND THE CHRISTIAN RIGHT

Despite Bush's emphasis on the Jamestown venture as being somehow preordained by God, he was careful not to emphasize, or even
mention, the specifically Christian nature of the English venture at
Jamestown. One of the most notable examples of the diverse claims
made upon Jamestown as a national symbol is that of the Christian
nationalists. As Jamestown is upheld as a symbol of the nation, it is
not surprising that it gets caught up in the current religious politics
surrounding our national identity. The commemoration of Jamestown became yet another opportunity for the Christian right to de-
cry what it sees as an overly secular government and to portray the
U.S. as a nation where God is under attack—a nation that was once
close to God, but has since fallen from grace.

The Christian Law Association website (www.christianlaw.org)
featured an article entitled "Jamestown: Where America Became
a Christian Nation," which says that Jamestown "was dedicated to
God and to the expansion of the Christian faith" (CLA 2008). Lamenting the current situation, this article states, "Since appreciation
for both religion and patriotism has reached a low ebb in 2007, no
official government ceremonies commemorating the dedication of
our nation to God in 2007 are planned for the 400th anniversary of
Jamestown" (CLA 2008).

In response to the perceived exclusion of Christians from the
commemoration, an organization called Vision Forum Ministries
(2008) created "Jamestown Quadricentennial: A Celebration of
America's Providential History." The weeklong event was scheduled
to include everything from history tours to kiddie rides, firearms
demonstrations to Christian speakers. Pat Robertson also held his
own commemoration, and a Virginia megachurch held a conference
featuring a costumed reenactment of the original landing at which

the participants planted white crosses with "One Nation Under God" inscribed (Clarkson 2007). Clearly, the Christian nationalists are not interested in claiming religious freedom as an inheritance from our Jamestown ancestors.

The conflict over the rightful place of Christianity in a commemoration of Jamestown is but one aspect of the complexity of the commemoration in relation to our nation's diversity. For the remainder of the paper, I would like to say more about this diversity in the past and present, and how it has (and has not) been commemorated.

JAMESTOWN AND DIVERSITY: NATIVE AMERICANS AND AFRICAN AMERICANS

Another aspect of Americanness that has figured largely in the discourse of the 2007 Jamestown commemoration is the diversity of our country, a topic more avoided in the past. For the first time in the history of Jamestown commemorations, the diversity and complexity of cultural and ethnic interactions that was part of the Jamestown experience was well recognized. The Jamestown 400th Commemoration Commission Act of 2000 stated among its purposes: "to assist in ensuring that the Jamestown 2007 observances are inclusive and appropriately recognize the experiences of all people present in 17th century Jamestown." Members of the federal Commission and the Virginia-based Jamestown 2007 Steering Committee included Native Americans and African Americans; the primary educational exhibits and teaching materials about Jamestown addressed their experiences; and the "Signature Events" of the commemoration included a variety of events focused on these two groups.[2] In fact, the very use of the language of "commemoration," rather than "celebration," was a result of the inclusion of Native Americans in this process.

The specifically Native American and African American events that were part of the commemoration included symposia, museum displays, educational programs, and media events. Broadly, these addressed the place of Native Americans and African Americans in the past and how that experience relates to the present. For example, PBS television host Tavis Smiley led his annual State of the Black Union address in Virginia in 2007, bringing together African American notables to explore "The African American Imprint on America." In conjunction with the commemoration events at Jamestown, events were also held in other Virginia locales, including an American Indian Intertribal Festival, as well as a Virginia Black Expo.

In his remarks, even President Bush acknowledged the troubling interactions of diverse groups in the colonial past. He said, "The expansion of Jamestown came at a terrible cost to the native tribes of the region, who lost their lands and their way of life. And for many Africans, the journey to Virginia represented the beginnings of a life of hard labor and bondage" (Bush 2007). The Queen herself echoed Bush, saying, "Human progress rarely comes without cost," and she noted the need to recognize the significance of Jamestown in relation to "when three great civilisations came together for the first time —Western European, Native American, and African" (Queen Elizabeth II 2007).

In all of these ways, the Jamestown Commemorations of 2007 clearly differed from past commemorations.[3] Jamestown became reconfigured as the birthplace not just of America, but of American diversity. In contrast, the Commemoration of 1957, at which the Queen also appeared, had been criticized for being a nearly all-White celebration (Rothstein 2007). In 1957, the State of Virginia was actively resisting the challenges of the Civil Rights Movement in ways that echoed in the Jamestown Commemoration. Circa 1957, Jamestown, as the birthplace of America, was the birthplace of a people who still then largely equated their national identity with race.

This embrace of the Native American and African place in the colonial experience was not without its critics from diverse perspectives. An essay in the *National Review* (Kavulla 2007) lamented that Native Americans were incorrectly portrayed as passive victims in the commemoration events and complained that African Americans were overrepresented in the commemoration in that their numbers were relatively few until the latter part of the 17th century. The conservative media organization *World Net* posted an article criticizing President Bush and the Queen for having "jumped onto the politically correct bandwagon" for acknowledging the diversity of the past (Unruh 2007). Peter Brimelow's anti-immigrant website *V-Dare. com*, includes several articles from Pat Buchanan and others criticizing the representations of diversity in the recent Jamestown commemoration. An article by Allan Wall (2007), entitled "Memo from Mexico, Celebrate (Don't Just "Commemorate") Jamestown!," expresses concern that four hundred years after the English settlement in Jamestown first helped keep the Spanish at bay, "Spanish-speakers may yet grab the whole territory—through immigration."

Alternatively, more radical Native American and African American groups, such as the American Indian Movement and the New Black Panther Party, considered the commemoration a whitewash of history and a glorification of European colonialism (Zander 2007). The website stolencontinent.org ridiculed the Native American groups that performed for the Queen and argued that as an alternative to such commemorations there should be international days of remembrance akin to Jewish remembrances of the Holocaust (Cordova 2008).

JAMESTOWN AND DIVERSITY: LATIN AMERICANS AND ASIAN AMERICANS

While some have criticized the extent to which diversity was celebrated at Jamestown, I actually would like to argue that the commemoration of Jamestown could and perhaps should have been even more inclusive. My simple point is that if Jamestown's significance is as a national symbol, and if democracy is what gives that symbol meaning, then why not expand the telling of the story in a way that better represents and incorporates the people of our contemporary nation? To do so is not simply to add another "me too" to the multicultural list, but rather to speak more to the complexity of the context of Jamestown in ways that are historically accurate and also allow for the telling of an even more complex and relevant story.

As I have already noted, the diversity represented in the Jamestown Commemoration of 2007 was a corrective to exclusions of 1957 and earlier. I suggest, however, that in making this corrective the Jamestown Commemoration of 2007 in some ways ignored the America that it should reflect today. Since 1957, we have seen movements of civil rights and human rights, Black Power and Red Power. Now, the cultural and ethnic politics of 2007 are more about immigration and other global flows, about Minutemen and English Only proposals, about Chinese capital and jobs in India, and about religious fundamentalists abroad and in our heartland. The origin story that we create about Jamestown needs to address these new forms of diversity and these new global challenges that we confront and that we seek to understand.

Specifically, what is missing most from the official commemorations, discussions, and celebrations at early Jamestown is mention of Asians and Latin Americans. This is, of course, appropriate to a degree, since there were neither Asians nor Latinos in great numbers at Jamestown. However, if Jamestown is to be offered as a symbol of our nation, as a place where the qualities of our nation that we cherish today had their origins, then I argue that it would be appropriate to give these places and peoples more mention.[4]

I see in the commemoration of Jamestown an opportunity to explore some peculiar conjunctures between the past and the present—conjunctures which perhaps give us a different way of looking at Jamestown and a different way of looking at our diversity in the present. In a certain sense, in 1607 at Jamestown we see some English-speaking, Christian, Protestant men, struggling to stake out a claim to territory and identity, fearful of the spread of Spanish speakers, mostly Catholic, to the South and West. Sound familiar? We can also see Jamestown 1607 as a step in part of a longer process of wealthy White folks looking to maximize their economic opportunity through connections with Asia. Sound familiar again? I think these characterizations of Jamestown in and after 1607 speak in some important ways to the U.S. in 2007. If we can acknowledge that from our earliest days, from the very beginning of our story as a people, Latinos and Asians played a part, then we have a different story of our past and a different understanding of our present. I think a story of the past that is relevant today is that by 1607 there had been more Spanish descended folks in the landmass that became the U.S. than there were English.[5] Also, while Asians did not play as significant a role, there were at least a few South Asians in Jamestown by the 1620s, and the dream that brought the English to Jamestown, was at least partly a dream about Asia (Assisi 2007).

Expanding the American origin story as told through Jamestown is perhaps most important because for the past thirty years or so Latinos and Asians have been the fastest-growing populations in the U.S., and throughout the South as well (Bernstein 2004). The Census

Bureau's 2006 American Community Survey estimates that persons of Hispanic or Latino origin represent about 15 percent of the population, and Asians approximately 5 percent; and nearly 1 in 5 Americans above the age of 5 speaks a language other than English at home. In considering these numbers, national celebrations of Englishness should seem peculiar and will continue to seem increasingly so. I suggest that the Jamestown Commemoration of 2057 will need to speak a different language, metaphorically at least, if it is to communicate a meaningful origin story to a changing nation.[6]

NOTES

1. While numerous scholars across diverse disciplines have documented this diversity, this paper was particularly influenced by *Cultural Diversity in the U.S. South, Anthropological Contributions to a Region in Transition, Southern Anthropological Society Proceedings, No. 31*, edited by Carole E. Hill and Patricia D. Beaver.

2. For a list of the commission members see http://www. jametown2007.org/who-federaljamestowncommission.cfm. For Steering Committee members see http://www.jamestown2007.org/who-jamestownsteeringcommittee.cfm. For a list of the Signature Events see http://www.jamestown2007.org/se-signature-eventslist.cfm. For other related commemoration events see http://www. historyisfun.org/special-programs.htm. To see the curriculum created around Jamestown 400 see http://www.jamestownjourney. org/Home.htm. For a discussion of the more inclusive exhibits at Jamestown see Rothstein (2007).

3. Previous celebrations have incorporated non-Whites as participants and visitors, but they have not emphasized diversity as a central American value with its beginnings at Jamestown (Gleach 2003).

4. It is interesting to note that even Polish Americans sought to use the Jamestown Commemoration as an opportunity to emphasize their place in the American fabric. The President of the Polish American Congress and Polish National Alliance encouraged Polonia organizations "to inform and teach others why we commemorate the establishment of a Nation and the contribution of those first Polish pioneers and the beginning of an American Polonia" (Spula 2007).

5. Interestingly, as I was working on this paper, the Berry Site of North Carolina, studied by David Moore of Warren Wilson College and others, was featured on a UNC-TV segment "Exploring North Carolina." The site includes remains of a mid-16th-century Spanish fort in the foothills of the Smoky Mountains, many years before the settlement of Jamestown.

6. Commemorations are, of course, political—they are selective, and laden with complex meanings, and therefore require ongoing critical inquiry. I hope that my comments are a useful contribution to this inquiry and do nothing to diminish the intelligence, creativity, and good will that clearly informed the recent Jamestown commemorations.

WORKS CITED

Assisi, Francis C. 2007. Earliest Asian Immigrants in America: South Asians In Colonial Virginia (Part1). http://www.indolink.com/displayArticleS. php?id=051307084810.

Association for the Preservation of Virginia Antiquities (APVA). 2000. History of Jamestown. http://www.apva.org/history/.

Anderson, Benedict. 1991[1983]. *Imagined Communities: Reflections on the Origins and Spread of Nationalism*. London: Verso.

Barthes, Roland. 1972. *Mythologies*. London: Paladin.

Bernstein, Robert. 2004. Hispanic and Asian Americans Increasing
    Faster Than Overall Population. US Census Bureau News.
    Washington DC. http://www.census.gov/Press-Release/www/
    releases/archives/ race/ 001839.html.

Bush, George W. 2007. President Bush Celebrates America's 400th
    Anniversary in Jamestown. http://www.whitehouse.gov/
    news/releases/2007/05/ 20070513.html.

Christian Law Association (CLA). 2007. Jamestown: Where America
    Became a Christian Nation. http://www.christianlaw.org/
    index.php/articles/jamestown.html.

Clarkson, Frederick. 2007. History is Powerful: Why the Christian
    Right Distorts History and Why it Matters. *Public Eye
    Magazine*. Spring. http://www.publiceye.org/magazine/
    v21n2/history.html.

Cordova, Carlos. 2008. Jamestown: Commemorating 400 years of
    English Genocide and Colonization.
    http://www.stolencontinent.org/jamestown.htm.

Gleach, Frederic W. 2003. "Pocahontas at the Fair: Crafting Identities
    at the 1907 Jamestown Exposition." *Ethnohistory* 50(3): 419-
    445.

Hill, Carole E. and Patricia D. Beaver, eds. 1998. *Cultural Diversity
    in the U.S. South, Anthropological Contributions to a Region
    in Transition.* Southern Anthropological Society Proceedings,
    No. 31. Athens: University of Georgia Press.

Hobsbawm, Eric. 1983. "Introduction: Inventing Traditions." In *The
    Invention of Tradition*, edited by E. Hobsbawm and T.
    Ranger, 1-14. New York: Cambridge University Press.

Horn, James. 2006. *Land as God Made It: Jamestown and the Birth of
    America*. New York: Basic Books.

Jamestown 400th Commemoration Commission Act of 2000. Pub.
L. 106–565. 114 Stat. 2812 (2000).

Kavulla, Travis. 2007. "Jamestown in the American Eye: A Colony
and its Commemorations." *National Review* LIX(10), June
11.

Kelso, William M. 2006. *Jamestown, the Buried Truth*. Charlottesville: University of Virginia Press.

Kupperman, Karen Ordahl. 2007. *The Jamestown Project*.
Cambridge: Belknap Press of Harvard University Press.

Melomo, Vincent H. 1994. *Historical or Archaeological Questions?
The Protohistoric Period in Sonora, Mexico*. Master's thesis,
Binghamton University (SUNY).

———. 2003. *Immigrant Dreams and Second Generation Realities:
Indian Americans Negotiating Marriage, Culture and Identity
in North Carolina in Late Modernity*. PhD diss., Binghamton
University (SUNY).

Price, David A. 2005. *Love and Hate in Jamestown: John Smith, Pocahontas, and the Heart of a New Nation*. New York: Alfred A.
Knopf.

Queen Elizabeth II. 2007. Text of The Queen's speech at the State
Capitol in Richmond, Virginia, United States of America.
3 May. http://www.royal.gov.uk/output/Page5961.asp.

Rothstein, Edward. 2007. "Captain Smith, the Tides are Shifting on
the James." *The New York Times*. March 2. http://travel.
nytimes.com/2007/03/02/arts/ design/02jame.html.

Rountree, Helen C. 2006. *Pocahontas, Powhatan, Opechancanough:
Three Indian Lives Changed by Jamestown*. Charlottesville:
University of Virginia Press.

Spula, Frank J. 2007. A Jamestown Appeal.
http://www.polamcon.org/ jamestown/index.htm.

Unruh, Bob. 2007. Historic Jamestown Marks 400 Years since 'Invasion.' http://www.worldnetdaily.com/news/article. asp?ARTICLE_ID=54603.

Vision Forum Ministries. 2008. Jamestown Quadricentennial: A Celebration of America's Providential History. http://www. visionforumministries.org/events/jq/.

Wall, Allan. 2007. Memo From Mexico, Celebrate (Don't Just Commemorate) Jamestown! http://www.vdare.com/ awall/070502_memo.htm.

Woolley, Benjamin. 2008. *Savage Kingdom: The True Story of Jamestown, 1607, and the Settlement of America*. New York: Harper Collins.

Zander, Carly. 2007. Media Advisory: Jamestown Settlement Denies Free Speech Permit to Black/Indian Jamestown Opponents. http://www.send2press.com/newswire/2007-05-0503-005. shtml.

Vandalizing Meaning, Stealing Memory: Thoughts on Crimes in Galleries and Museums*

Avi Brisman, Emory University

INTRODUCTION

In March 2008, the industrial rock group Nine Inch Nails, fronted by Trent Reznor, released *Ghosts I-IV*, an album of thirty-six near-instrumental tracks. Critical response to the album was mixed, but generally favorable, with one critic labeling it "engrossing and encompassing" (Thompson 2008a) and another referring to it as an "absorbing musical experience" (Walls 2008), with a third lamenting that it "feels emaciated and half-finished" (Briehan 2008). Given such comments, it would be hard to imagine the album generating much interest outside of the rock world; and it would seem an unlikely subject for the start to an academic paper—even in a field as broad and accommodating as anthropology. But what has garnered the attention of various news agencies, as well as of this author, is that Mr. Reznor gave the music a Creative Commons license, rather than a standard copyright, meaning that it may be shared, altered, reworked, and remixed as long as the music built on *Ghosts* is non

*Originally published as "Vandalizing Meaning, Stealing Memory: Artistic, Cultural, and Theoretical Implications of Crime in Galleries and Museums," in *Critical Criminology* 19, no. 1 (2011): 15-28. Reprinted with kind permission from Springer Science+Business Media B.V.: http://www.springer.com/ social+sciences/criminology/journal/10612 Abstract: http://www.springerlink. com/content/0486478057713qm6/

commercial and attributed to Nine Inch Nails (see, e.g., Briehan 2008; Deeds 2008; Jolley 2008; Lomax 2008; Norris 2008; Pareles 2008; Thompson 2008a; Van Buskirk 2008a; Walls 2008; Worthen 2008).

Coming a year after Radiohead's 2007 pay-what-you-want digital release of *In Rainbows*, Nine Inch Nails' digital release of *Ghosts* may be a harbinger of musical distribution.[1] But Nine Inch Nails' blurring the lines between artist and audience—its effective encouragement of appropriation, theft, and vandalism of its own work—is hardly a new phenomenon. Indeed, in the visual arts, this kind of "collaborative" endeavor has a rich history. For example, in 1953, Robert Rauschenberg produced *Erased de Kooning Drawing* by taking a drawing already made by Willem de Kooning—which de Kooning had given him—erasing it, framing it, and announcing that he had created a new artwork altogether.[2] More recently, Felix Gonzalez-Torres created *Untitled (Placebo)* (1991), consisting of 1,200 pounds (roughly 40,000 pieces) of silver-wrapped candy arranged as a carpet on museum gallery floors. *Untitled (Placebo)* has been installed in a number of venues.[3] For each installation, visitors are invited to take a piece of candy; in doing so, they alter the visual appearance of the candy carpet and contribute to the slow disappearance of the sculpture over the course of the exhibition.[4]

But where Nine Inch Nails and Gonzalez-Torres have facilitated the taking, remaking, remixing (or eating, in the case of the latter) of their art—and where Rauschenberg reworked de Kooning's drawing with the latter's assent—in this paper, I focus on instances where such use constitutes *misuse* or *abuse*—where such acts are considered theft or vandalism—because the acts are uninvited (and usually unappreciated). I offer representative examples (rather than an exhaustive account) of both works that have been stolen and vandalized. First, I explore the extent to which theft may affect our consideration, understanding, and memory of a given work of art (regardless of whether the object is ultimately recovered) as well as our experience of the museum in which the work is housed (especially if efforts are subsequently undertaken to improve security, as with the Munch Museum following the theft of *Scream* and *Madonna*). Next, I turn to vandalism and examine whether and how such acts subsequently affect our consideration, understanding, and memory of the works as art objects. Contemplating theft and vandalism together, I argue that how we regard such events should be determined not by their criminality, but by the perpetrators' intent and the effect of the acts on the meaning and memory of the works.

STEALING MEMORY

Edvard Munch's Scream *(1893) and* Madonna *(1893-94)*

On August 22, 2004, two masked armed robbers burst into the Munch Museum in Oslo, Norway, and stole the museum's *Scream*, along with Munch's *Madonna*, in plain view of museum visitors. The expressionist masterpieces were recovered in August 2006, but both were damaged (Van Gelder 2007a). Blaming lax security, the Munch Museum closed for ten months for a multi-million dollar security overhaul. Today, visitors pass through metal detectors and must place their bags and personal items through a scanning device before arriving at the ticket booth, where they then must pass through a second metal detector; security cameras and guards also monitor the museum (Agence France Presse 2008).

The theft of the Munch Museum's *Scream* and *Madonna* has most probably affected the experience of visitors to the museum. Those who have visited the museum prior to the theft will undoubtedly notice the heightened security measures. Those new to the museum but who have learned about the revamped security may well contemplate these features. Only those without prior exposure to the museum and knowledge of the theft and ensuing overhaul may be unaffected by the double metal detectors, scanning device, security cameras, and increased guard presence.

Whether the theft of the Munch Museum's *Scream* and *Madonna* has shaped the experience of the paintings themselves is a different matter. Again, I believe that knowledge of the theft may play a role, altering how one interacts with the paintings. For example, some may choose to look at these paintings precisely *because* they were stolen and the theft, recovery, and restoration were much publicized. Others may be drawn to them for reasons entirely unrelated to the theft, such as their lurid colors or art-historical significance, but they may find themselves unable to contemplate the works divorced from the fact of their theft. Some people may be able to overlook or ignore the influence of the theft; for many, the theft may become part of the works of art (apart from the mere visual indicia of the theft that restoration efforts could not correct, such as scratches, tears, and signs of dampness).

On some level, then, the theft of the Munch Museum's *Scream* and *Madonna*—an act of disrespect and desecration—has produced the reverse effect—increasing the significance and allure of the paintings. Whereas before the theft, gaining entrance to the Munch Museum and audience with the *Scream* and *Madonna* was relatively easy, today the paintings are guarded, like a political leader or some other V.I.P. Experiencing the *Scream* and *Madonna* now requires negotiating metal detectors, carrying out the performance of being screened, and subjecting one's self to constant surveillance.

In a slightly different vein, one could argue that the 2004 theft has not transformed the *Scream* and *Madonna* from art objects to cultural icons but has simply continued a process begun years before. In 1983-84, Andy Warhol made a series of silk prints of works by Munch, which included prints of *Scream*. Although Warhol's idea was to desacralize Munch's *Scream* by mass-producing its likeness—something that Warhol was known for doing with other works and images of famous people—Munch himself had already taken such steps by making multiple versions of *Scream*, as well as lithographs of the work for reproduction.[5] Over the years, *Scream* has been further reproduced—and, hence, further desacralized—by appearing on T-shirts, coffee mugs, and inflatable punching bags and by being featured in episodes of *The Simpsons* and *Beavis and Butt-head*. In addition, the film director Wes Craven has given the antagonist of his *Scream* horror films, Ghostface, a white mask inspired by the central figure in Munch's *Scream*. Even the 2004 theft of *Scream* may be considered a "reproduction" of sorts: the National Gallery of Norway's *Scream* was stolen on February 14, 1994 (during the Winter Olympics in Lillehammer), and recovered on May 7, 1994.

With this perspective in mind, every act of desacralization to *Scream* as a work of art—be it visual or larcenous reproduction—ironically elevates its status as a cultural icon. Whether future thefts of *Scream* will occur because the work of art is now a cultural icon and thus an appealing target or because *Scream* has become so mass-produced and quotidian that it is no longer viewed as a sacred work of art, but as a form of communal property, remains to be seen. The point is that a tension surrounds *Scream*, with the fact of its previous theft(s) and potential for future theft(s) affecting its meaning as well as individuals' experiences (and memories of their experiences) of it.

Leonardo da Vinci's Mona Lisa *(c. 1503-06)*

Stolen in 1911 and struck by a stone in 1956, Leonardo's sixteenth-century portrait *Mona Lisa* (also known as *La Gioconda* or *La Jaconde*) now rests in a sealed enclosure behind 1.52-inch-thick glass at a permanent temperature of 43 degrees Fahrenheit and 50 percent humidity in the Musée du Louvre in Paris, France (Riding 2005, 2006). The "world's most famous painting" is further protected by a wooden fence that prevents the approximately six-and-a-half million people who view the painting each year from venturing too close to it (Sassoon 2001). (The Louvre estimates that eighty percent of its visitors come specifically to see the *Mona Lisa* (Riding 2005).)

Like Munch's *Scream*, one could argue that Leonardo's *Mona Lisa* has also undergone a transformation from work of art to cultural icon. Again, Warhol has played a role in this process. In 1963, he made a series of serigraph prints of Lisa Gherardini, wife of Francesco del Giocondo—the subject of da Vinci's painting. Again, Warhol's desire was to desacralize the painting. And like *Scream*, desacralization of *Mona Lisa* by mass reproduction had already occurred (although unlike *Scream*, the process did not begin with the original artist). In the nineteenth century, the painting gained fame as it was reproduced in lithographs, postcards, and photographs. In 1919, Marcel Duchamp created a work, *L.H.O.O.Q.*, depicting the woman with a moustache—a piece that I will discuss in greater detail below. Salvador Dali painted himself as Mona Lisa in 1954 and both Jasper Johns and Robert Rauschenberg integrated the image of Mona Lisa into their works.[6] Endless depictions, appropriations, and permutations of Mona Lisa appear on the website Megamonalisa.com.

According to Sassoon (2001), however, the theft and subsequent recovery of *Mona Lisa* in 1911—both of which "unleashed a swarm of newspaper features, commemorative postcards, cartoons, ballads, cabaret-revues and comic silent films"—clinched her international celebrity and spurred the subsequent renditions by Duchamp, Warhol, and others (Nicholl 2002). Regardless of the initial catalyst— regardless of whether mass reproduction forged the path to theft or theft spurred mass reproduction—the theft of *Mona Lisa*, like that of *Scream*, has affected the experience of the museum and the painting.

First, while visitors to the Louvre may not contemplate the fact of *Mona Lisa's* theft—indeed, they may not even know that it was once stolen—its theft in 1911 has contributed to its celebrity and many may wish to see it just because it is famous. Second, that the painting has been stolen and is now roped off and placed behind glass dictates the nature of the interaction with it. Viewers must experience it from afar; that it may be seen, but not approached, contributes to its status and allure, while diminishing the visceral impact and intellectual stimulus that accompanies close examination and interaction with a work of art.

All in all, like *Scream*, one could argue that whatever significance *Mona Lisa* might have had as an artistic innovation (such as its avoidance of sharp outlines and the sitter's direct engagement with the viewer) has been overshadowed. If it has any connection to art (other than being a painting in a museum), it symbolizes *art* as a whole, while ceasing to be a specific (or singular) *work* of art with which individuals may have an intimate visual or spiritual experience.

Vandalizing Meaning

While the theft of works of art may transform the experience of the museum from which they were stolen and, if recovered, the experience of the objects themselves when re-exhibited, the vandalization of works on view in museums and galleries can also have an effect on the meaning and memory of and meaning and memories associated with a work of art. I distinguish here based on intent, addressing first the willful defacement or destruction of works of art for mischievous or malicious reasons and then turning to the defacement or destruction of works of art as artistic statements.

Attack on Art, Attack on Memory

On Sunday, October 7, 2007, during the yearly all-night festival of arts and music (called "the White Night") in Paris, France, four men and one woman, apparently drunk, broke into the Musée d'Orsay. One of the intruders punched an impressionist masterpiece— Claude Monet's *Le Pont d'Argenteuil* (*The Bridge at Argenteuil*) (1874)—leaving a four-inch tear (Almendros 2007; Kanter 2007a; see also Kanter 2007b). Christine Albanel, Minister of Culture, referred to the break-in as "an attack against our memory and our heritage" and lamented the recent spate of attacks on works of art in France, including a January 2006 assault on Duchamp's *Fountain* (1917/1964) while it was on view as part of the "Dada" exhibition at the Pompidou Center in Paris; and to an incident in July 2007 in Avignon, where a woman left a red, lip-shaped smear on an untitled immaculate white canvas by the American artist Cy Twombly (Kanter 2007a). Albanel also promised improved security at French museums and called for stronger sanctions for those who desecrate French monuments, institutions, and works of art (Kanter 2007a).

It remains to be seen how viewers will respond to *Le Pont d'Argenteuil* after it is repaired and re-exhibited in a more heavily guarded Musée d'Orsay. My hunch is that the effect of the attack on *Le Pont d'Argenteuil* will be similar to the effect of the theft of *Scream* and *Madonna*, with some visitors oblivious of the fact of its attack; some aware of, but able to overlook or ignore, the fact of its attack; some drawn to the piece because of the attack; and some unable to divorce the fact of the attack from the work as an art object and as a renowned example of impressionism. But when attacks are perpetrated as performance pieces—when artists attack other artists' works of art—when vandalism becomes a medium of expression, rather than a mere example of hooliganism—the range of potential meanings and memories becomes greater. Examining both the attack on Duchamp's *Fountain* and the assault on Twombly's untitled white canvas, I argue below that Albanel errs in categorizing these incidents with the vandalism of *Le Pont d'Argenteuil*.

VANDALISM AS A(N) (ARTISTIC) STATEMENT/VANDALISM IN THE NAME OF ART/VANDALISM AS ART

If and when the untitled Twombly piece is re-exhibited, it will very likely raise the questions noted above about the extent to which an experience of it can divorced from the kiss. But given that Sam kissed the painting as an "artistic act" and as a means of *interacting* with the artist and the work, rather than defacing it or destroying it, the potential meaning of the work is broadened. Aside from the aesthetics of the kiss (the smeared lipstick is actually a visually intriguing gesture or form), one must consider how else Sam could have acted. How else could she have expressed her love? Could she have given the painting a rose? Could she have hugged it or caressed it? Could she have taken it home—stolen it? Given the conceptual nature of Sam's kiss, is it really an artistic act—or a successful artistic act—if she "wasn't thinking"? What do we make of the fact that the alleged artistic act was not even original? (In 1977, Ruth van Herpen kissed a white monochrome painting by Jo Baer in the Oxford Museum of Art, smearing lipstick across it and claiming "[The work] looked so cold. I only kissed it to cheer it up" (Althouse 2007).

The extent to which Sam intended to engage van Herpen and Baer, in addition to Twombly, is unknown, as is the question of whether Twombly indeed "understood," as Sam claims he would have. The larger point is that vandalism for vandalism's sake can, like the theft of a work of art, affect the meaning and memory of the work and the institution in which it is housed; vandalism for art's sake, unlike the theft of a work of art (unless the theft is considered a work of art), further expands the potential meaning and memory of the work.

On January 4, 2006, the seventy-seven-year-old French performance artist Pierre Pinoncelli attacked Duchamp's *Fountain* (a piece
consisting solely of a flipped-upside-down urinal) with a small hammer, causing it to be chipped (*Duchamp's Dada Pissoir Attacked* 2006;
Jagvonjeul n.d.; Riding 2006).[8]

Pinoncelli was arrested at the scene and subsequently received a
fine of approximately $262,000 and a suspended prison term for the
self-described destructive "happening" (*Duchamp's Dada Pissoir Attacked* 2006; Riding 2006).

This was not the first time that Pinoncelli had targeted
Duchamp's *Fountain*. Indeed, much as the *Fountain* in the Pompidou is a replica of the original, made in 1917, Pinoncelli's attack in
2006 replicated or repeated an earlier attack on the same urinal. In
1993, when the Pompidou *Fountain* was on view at Carré d'Art in
Nimes, Pinoncelli urinated in it and also attacked it with a hammer,
for which he received a fine of roughly $37,500 and a sentence of one
month's imprisonment for "voluntary degradation of an object of
public utility" (see *Duchamp's Dada Pissoir Attacked* 2006; Jagvonjeul n.d.; Riding 2006). In his defense, Pinoncelli claimed, much as
Sam did with respect to her kiss of Twombly's painting, that "Duchamp would have understood. I gave back to the *Fountain* its original
purpose" and that he (Pinoncelli) wanted "to rescue the work from
its inflated iconic status and return it to its original function as a urinal" (*Duchamp's Dada Pissoir Attacked* 2006; Jagvonjeul n.d.).

Chances are that Duchamp probably would have "understood"
Pinoncelli's attacks because Duchamp's whole purpose in "creating" *Fountain*, which he signed "R. Mutt," was to ignite debate surrounding the question, "What is art?" and to underscore his point
that artists determine what constitutes art. Thus, one could maintain
that Pinoncelli's action engages Duchamp and carries on his spirit—more convincingly, at least, than the argument that Sam's kiss

converses with Twombly or that the assault on *Le Pont d'Argenteuil* communicates with Monet. But I contend that closer artistic scrutiny of Pinoncelli's "performance pieces" calls into question their effectiveness of as works of art.

First, while urinating in a urinal that has been turned upside-down and labeled *Fountain* may return the urinal to its original purpose, attacking it with a hammer makes less sense. Hitting *Fountain* and chipping it seems more like an aggressive attempt to leave a permanent mark on the work, rather than clear and coherent artistic expression. If urinating in the urinal did not sufficiently satisfy Pinoncelli's desire to return the urinal to its original purpose, could he not have tried attaching plumbing to *Fountain*? What about placing a urinal deodorizing block (also known as a deodorizing urinal cake) in *Fountain*—perhaps to suggest that this work of art "stinks"? Given that individuals rarely attack urinals that appear in restrooms with hammers, it is hard to understand how hitting *Fountain* (an upside-down urinal appearing in a gallery) returns the urinal to its original function.

Second, while Pinoncelli claimed to have wanted to "rescue the work from its inflated iconic status," in light of the thefts of *Scream* and the theft and vandalism of *Mona Lisa*, it would seem that Pinoncelli's action achieved precisely the opposite effect—further inflating its iconic status. The original *Fountain* was deemed neither original nor art when Duchamp offered it for the first exhibition of the Society of Independent Artists in New York in 1917. What better way to elevate the iconic status of *Fountain* than with a high-publicity attack causing damage to the urinal—damage necessitating restoration by art restoration experts, rather than by plumbers? If rescuing the work from its "inflated iconic status" was Pinoncelli's goal, then would not subtly replacing *Fountain* with another urinal—perhaps one from the restroom at the Pompidou Center—have more successfully achieved his stated intent? Given that vandalism to ordinary urinals does not garner media attention and fines of $10,000 or $100,000, it would seem that Pinoncelli selected precisely the wrong way to desacralize the work.

Finally, while Duchamp might have understood Pinoncelli's attacks as Dadaist performances, it seems that a far more compelling conversation might have unfolded between Pinoncelli and Duchamp had the former contemplated the latter's own efforts at desacralization. As noted above, Duchamp's *L.H.O.O.Q.* involved taking an "objet trouvé" (a found object)—in this case, a cheap postcard reproduction of da Vinci's *Mona Lisa*—drawing a mustache and beard on the woman's face, and changing the title.[9] While Duchamp could have vandalized the original *Mona Lisa*, his Dadaist attempt to destroy conventional notions of art proved far more successful by taking a pedestrian object—a postcard—a reproduction of a work of art, rather than a work itself—and rendering it art by altering it slightly and renaming it. In other words, Duchamp understood that attacking conventional notions of art would (need to) entail symbolic gestures to convert utilitarian objects into art objects, rather than actual acts of violence that would simply transform art objects into damaged or destroyed art objects.[10] To rescue *Fountain* from its inflated iconic status—to return the urinal from a work of art to an ordinary utilitarian object—Pinoncelli would have needed to have engaged in a symbolic gesture like Duchamp's with *L.H.O.O.Q.*

In sum, Pinoncelli's attacks or performance pieces illustrate how vandalism for art's sake can add another element or layer of meaning to the assaulted object. But like Sam's kiss, Pinoncelli's self-proclaimed tributes to Duchamp highlight how "art vandalism" may not necessarily make good art—art that is, among other things, conceptually coherent, tight, and memorable art.

In order to further understand my last point—that vandalism for art's sake may add another element or layer of meaning to the assaulted object, but may not produce compelling art in and of itself—consider Kazmir Malevich's *Suprematisme 1920-1927* (also known as *White Cross on Gray* (1921)), an oil on canvas painting depicting a white cross on a light grey background, that Alexander Brener, a thirty-nine-year-old Russian performance artist damaged in 1997. On Saturday, January 4, 1997, Brener sprayed a green dollar sign over fellow Russian Malevich's painting while it was being exhibited at the Stedelijk Museum of Modern Art, Amsterdam, Netherlands. Brener surrendered himself to museum authorities, explaining that he intended the dollar sign to appear nailed to the cross, and demanding that his work be viewed as a protest against "corruption and commercialism in the art world"—and, as such, performance art (Art Crimes n.d.; see also Cash 1998). Brener claimed that "[the] cross is a symbol of suffering, the $ a symbol of trade and merchandise. On humanitarian grounds are the ideas of Jesus Christ of higher significance of those of the money. What I did WAS NOT against the painting, I view my act as a dialogue with Malewitz" (Art Crimes n.d.). He further asserted that:

> the borders of art are sharply defined: art uses symbolic language and art is not allowed to harm people bodily. My act wasn't violent but symbolic. Other artists are predecessors. I did not surpass any border. Art has its own: artists have agreed themselves about what is acceptable: e.g., Sagrese in the 70s with Picasso's *Guernica* made a protest against the Vietnam War. Now he is a member of the establishment. I know I will be part of it once too. My target was real communication between people. (Force Mental 2005)

Brener was put on trial at the Criminal Court of Amsterdam, with the city of Amsterdam claiming that Brener had caused permanent damage and a loss of one-quarter of the market value of the painting (Art Crimes n.d.).[11] On Feb. 26, 1997, the Criminal Court of Amsterdam sentenced Brener to ten months of imprisonment, of which five months were suspended with time spent in pre-trial detention subtracted. He was also given two years of probation, during which time he was prohibited from entering the Stedelijk Museum (Art Crimes n.d.).[12]

Like Sam and Pinoncelli, Brener maintained that his attack/performance piece was an attempt to engage in a dialogue with the original artist. While Brener asserted that his act was symbolic, thereby couching it in Duchampian or Dadaist terms, it is hard to fully understand his argument in this respect. Admittedly, Brener did not slash Malevich's painting, the way Gerard Jan van Bladeren knifed Barnett Newsman's 8 x 18-foot blue monochrome *Cathedra* 1951. But despite the fact that both the cross and the dollar sign ($) serve as symbols, it is difficult to comprehend how *spray-painting* Malevich's canvas is symbolic or for what the vandalization serves as a symbol.

As with Sam and Pinoncelli, my sense is that Brener could have produced a "better" or "more successful" work of performance art. For instance, if one of his purposes was to engage in a dialogue with Malevich, he might have painted the $ in grey or white, rather than in green. Doing so would have produced a far more subtle effect and would have related more coherently to Malevich's aesthetic. If Brener wanted to call attention to the "corruption and commercialism in the art world" and to emphasize that stature is measured by dollar signs, he might have chosen to spray a dollar sign on one of Andy Warhol's dollar-sign paintings. (The dollar sign, like the Campbell's soup can, is a recurrent theme in Warhol's work, and with his dollar-sign paintings, Warhol undeniably signaled that "big-time art is big-time money" and that the sign for money as the sign for art (Gagosian Gallery 1997; see generally Hartocollis 2008).) Given Warhol's "in your face" message of commercialism conveyed in flamboyant colors, it seems that Brener might have created a more conceptually coherent and visually consistent work had he targeted Warhol with his green spray paint. In other words, critiquing Brener's attack/performance from an artistic point of view, one is left with the conclusion that he either picked the wrong color and medium (green spray paint) for his assault/performance piece or he selected the wrong work (Malevich's cross rather than Warhol's dollar sign). While his attack/performance—his spray painting a green dollar sign on Malevich's painting—adds another element or layer of meaning to Malevich's work, it is a shallow or thin layer—one that could have achieved greater depth or thickness with better conception and execution.

CONCLUSION

This paper has endeavored to show that two types of ostensibly straightforward criminal acts—theft and vandalism—affect and complicate how we understand, interpret, and remember the works of art that we view and the institutions in which they are exhibited. With respect to theft, it is difficult to argue that the theft of a work of art constitutes a work of art. (Perhaps that is why no one, to my knowledge, has made such a claim and perhaps this is why marginal works of art are rarely stolen.) Nevertheless, theft has an impact on the experience of the work and the museum. The theft of a work of art can change the work of art, rendering the work "the piece that was stolen," rather than a piece that is "good," "interesting," "inspiring," "stimulating," and so on; the theft of a work of art can also produce changes in the museum, transforming the museum from a temple or shrine, where intimate interaction with works is facilitated, to a fortress or zoo, where the objects are (literally) placed behind bars.

With respect to vandalism, we encounter instances in which the defacement of works of art are (allegedly) intended as artistic statements. While symbolic assaults, such as *L.H.O.O.Q.*, are often more successful artistic endeavors than actual ones, such as Sam's kiss, the bottom line is that assaults in the name of art further complicate the meaning and experience of the works and the venues in which they are viewed. This is not to suggest that individuals *should* engage in theft or vandalism of works of art. The only position I take in this regard is that if a theft or assault is to occur in the name of art, it should be well-conceived, well-executed, conceptually coherent, and aesthetically tight—like any work of art—in order to garner acceptance rather than (criminal) condemnation.

NOTES

1. On May 5, 2008, Nine Inch Nails released their latest album, *The Slip*, on their website. All ten tracks may be downloaded for free; and like *Ghosts I-IV*, *The Slip* was released under the Creative Commons "attribution noncommercial share-alike" license (see, e.g., Bateman 2008; Cromelin 2008; BBC News 2008; Malone 2008; Thompson 2008b; Van Buskirk 2008b).

2. Rauschenberg considered his ideas to be as interesting as drawings and *Erased de Kooning Drawing*, given to him by de Kooning specifically for the purpose of erasing it, is the visual result of Rauschenberg's idea.

3. Most recently, it appeared from December 1, 2007-March 23, 2008, at the Williams College Museum of Art in Williamstown, MA.

4. In another version of *Untitled (Placebo)*, the candy sits in a pile in the corner of the gallery, rather than as a carpet in the middle of the gallery floor. But the same principle applies: visitors are invited to take or eat pieces of the candy. Gonzalez-Torres created the piece as a

response to the AIDS epidemic and, in particular, to the death of his partner, Ross (Williams College Museum of Art 2007).

5. In addition to the Munch Museum's *Scream*, composed in oil, tempera, and pastel on cardboard, the National Gallery of Norway owns a painted version, as does the Norwegian billionaire, Petter Olsen. The Munch Museum apparently owns a second painted version of the *Scream*.

6. Jean-Michel Basquiat, who at times collaborated with Warhol, also adapted the portrait of Mona Lisa in his work.

7. Apparently, Sam also stated: "I stepped back. I found the painting even more beautiful. The artist left this white for me" (Van Gelder 2007b).

8. The Pompidou's *Fountain* is one of eight signed replicas made by Duchamp in 1964; the original *Fountain* was made in 1917 (see *Duchamp's Dada Pissoir Attacked* 2006; Jagvonjeul n.d.; Riding 2006).

9. *L.H.O.O.Q.*—the name of the Duchamp's piece—is a pun in French. When the letters are pronounced, they form a sentence—"Elle a chaud au cul"—loosely translated as "there is fire down below" and literally translated as "she is hot in the ass" (or "she has a hot ass"). (The slang term, "avoir chaud au cul," may be translated as "to be horny.") Part of Duchamp's intention here was to make reference to da Vinci's alleged homosexuality (see de Martino n.d.).

10. This distinction is understood quite well by Mike Bidlo, as evidenced by his series *Fountain Drawings* (1998) (see Brisman 1999).

11. According to Cash (1998), Malevich's painting was restored within months and re-exhibited.

12. Brener allegedly engaged in a hunger strike to protest what he perceived to be a harsh punishment (Art Crimes n.d.).

WORKS CITED

Agence France Presse. 2008. 'The Scream' to go Back on Display after 2004 Heist. Mar 3. http://news.yahoo.com/s/afp/20080303/ts_afp/ norwayartmunch.

Almendros, Cecile. 2007a. Intruders at Paris' Orsay Damage a Monet. *Associated Press.* Oct. 7. http://abcnews.go.com/Entertainment/wireStory?id=3699678.

Althouse, Ann. 2007. When I Kissed it, I Thought the Artist would Have Understood." Nov. 17. http://althouse.blogspot.com/2007/11/when-i-kissed-it-i-thought-artist-would.html.

Artcrimes. n.d. http://www.artcrimes.net/pages/malevich.html.

Bateman, Patrick. 2008. Review of *The Slip. SputnikMusic.* May 7. http://www.sputnikmusic.com/review_16134M.

BBC News. 2008. Nine Inch Nails Offer Free Album. BBC News. May 5. http://news.bbc.co.uk/1/hi/entertainment/7384324.stm.

Briehan, Tom. 2008. Review of *Ghosts I-IV. Pitchfork Record Review.* http://www.pitchforkmedia.com/article/record_review/49274-ghosts-i-iv.

Brisman, Avi. 1999. Re: Appropriation and Bidlo. Unpublished manuscript.

Cash, Stephanie. 1998. "Newman's *Cathedra* Slashed at Stedelijk." *Art in America* 86(1):27.

CBC News. 2007a. Kiss on $2.8M Painting More Than Just a Kiss. Oct. 9. http://www.cbc.ca/arts/artdesign/story/2007/10/09/kiss-painting.html.

————. 2007b. Artist Twombly Gets One Euro Award for Unwanted Kiss." Nov. 16. http://www.cbc.ca/arts/artdesign/story/2007/11/16/twomby-kiss.html.

Cromelin, Richard. 2008. "NIN's 'Slip' a Free Dive in Dark Waters." *Los Angeles Times*. May 7.

de Martino, Marco, n.d. Mona Lisa: Who Is Hidden Behind the Woman with the Mustache? Translated by Camillo Olivetti. http://www.artscienceresearchlab.org/articles/panorama.htm.

Deeds, Michael. 2008. "Review of *Ghosts I-IV.*" *Washington Post*. Mar. 27:C04.

"Duchamp's Dada Pissoir Attacked." 2006. *Art in America* 94(3):35.

Force Mental. 2005. http://www.clubmoral.com/forcemental/16/page.php?sid=139.

Gagosian Gallery. 1997. Press Release: Andy Warhol: Dollar Signs. Oct. 8. http://www.gagosian.com/exhibitions/beverly-hills-1997-11-andy-warhol.

Hartocollis, Anemona. 2008. "A Warhol Surfaces, Headed for Court." *The New York Times*. Feb. 19:A19.

Jagvonjeul, Kalitan. n.d. Under Destruction. *hEyOkA mAgAzInE*. http://www.heyokamagazine.com/HEYOKA.3.PINOCELLI.htm.

Jolley, John. 2008. Review of *Ghosts I-IV. Tiny Mix Tapes*. http://www.tinymixtapes.com/Nine-Inch-Nails,5829.

Kanter, James. 2007a. "Vandal Punches Hole in a Monet in Paris." *The New York Times*. Oct. 8:A8.

———. 2007b. "5 Held in Monet Attack." *The New York Times*. Oct. 11:B2.

Lomax, Alyce. 2008. Music Industry Gets Nailed Again. *The Motley Fool*. Mar. 4. http://www.fool.com/investing/general/2008/03/04/music-industry-gets-nailed-again.aspx.

Malone, Michael S. 2008. Will We Ever Pay for an Album Again? *ABC News*. May 9. http://abcnews.go.com/Business/story?id=4813233andpage=1.

Nicholl, Charles. 2002. The Myth of Mona Lisa. Review of *Mona Lisa: The History of the World's Most Famous Painting*. The Guardian. Mar. 28. http://books.guardian.co.uk/lrb/articles/0,6109,675653,00.html.

Norris, Chris. 2008. Review of *Ghosts I-IV. Blender*. http://www.blender.com/guide/reviews.aspx?id=5052.

Pareles, Jon. 2008. "Review of *Ghosts I-IV*." *The New York Times*. Mar. 10:B1, B6.

Riding, Alan. 2005. "In Louvre, New Room With View of 'Mona Lisa.'" *The New York Times*. Apr. 6.

———. 2006. "Conceptual Artist as Vandal: Walk Tall and Carry a Little Hammer (or Ax)." *The New York Times*. Jan. 7.

Sassoon, Donald. 2001. *Mona Lisa: The History of the World's Most Famous Painting*. New York: HarperCollins.

Thompson, Ed. 2008a. Review of *Ghosts I-IV. IGN*. Mar. 7. http://music.ign.com/articles/857/857752p1.html.

———. 2008b. Review of *The Slip*. May 7. xhttp://music.ign.com/articles/872/872307p1.html.

twosee. 2007. Cy Twombly. Nov. 26. http://twoseelife.blogspot.com/2007/11/cy-twombly.html.

Van Buskirk, Eliot. 2008a. "Nine Inch Nails Gets Creative With Radiohead-Style Release." *WIRED*. Mar. 3.

———. 2008b. "Nine Inch Nails Give Fans the Slip." *WIRED*. May 5.

Van Gelder, Lawrence. 2007a. "Arts, Briefly: Prison Sentences in Munch Thefts." *The New York Times*. Apr. 24:B2.

———. 2007b. "Arts, Briefly: Kiss for a Twombly Is A Case for the Police." *The New York Times*. July 23: B2.

———. 2007c. "Arts, Briefly: A Costly Kiss." *The New York Times*. Nov. 17:A20.

Walls, Seth Colter. 2008. "Nine Inch Nailed: How Artists' Online Distribution of Music (sorta) Works." *Newsweek*. Mar. 4.

Williams College Museum of Art. 2007. Press Release: Williams College Museum of Art Presents Felix Gonzalez-Torres *'Untitled' (Placebo)*. 1991: December 1, 2007-March 23, 2008. xhttp://www.wcma.org/press/07/07_ Felix_Gonzalez_ Torres.shtml.

Worthen, Ben. 2008. "Internet Lessons from Nine Inch Nails and Obama." *Wall Street Journal*. Mar. 3.

Menance and Majesty: The Jocassee Gorges Region of Upper South Carolina

John M. Coggeshall, Clemson University

INTRODUCTION

"Where the Blue Ridge yawns its greatness," my university's alma mater song opens in rising, majestic tones. Then, in contrast, hum the first few bars of "Dueling Banjos" from the film *Deliverance* and reflect upon what images come to mind. Conceiving the Jocassee Gorges area in the Blue Ridge Mountains of South Carolina as a majestic yet menacing "frontier space" encapsulates the deeply-rooted ambiguity of the place to residents and visitors alike. On a more fundamental level, as newcomers and old-timers battle to develop or preserve the area, this space becomes contested ground, representing the contrastive ideals of manicured fairways or timbered wilderness. Underlying this struggle is the cultural meaning of the land itself— to some a resource for "improvement," to others the symbolic connection to family, living and dead. This paper opens an exploration of these multiple and sometimes commingled interpretations of a well-known Southern landscape.

BACKGROUND

In this examination, my goal is to discover the various ways different groups conceptualize and utilize the same geographical space. How is it culturally possible that the same region can be both menacing and majestic, sometimes to the same groups of people? How do differing groups define the optimal use of this ambiguous space? How do these alternate uses intersect, overlap, or impede interconnected social places in kinship or symbolic systems? How do these physical and social relationships change over time? By examining narratives from local residents in Upstate South Carolina, I have initiated an explanation of the critical position of place, and the complex relationships between people and the spaces they occupy through time.

Contracted by the South Carolina Department of Natural Resources in August 2006 to work on a small grant project, I was originally expected to collect stories from the rapidly-disappearing "old time" Euro-American residents of the Jocassee Gorges region (upper Oconee and Pickens counties), abutting the border of the Carolinas. Soon I expanded the research to include newcomers living on the frontier, behind the palisaded walls of gated communities. Virtually invisible in the local histories have been African Americans, but I have contacted descendants of freed slaves settled among Euro-American residents. As much as possible, I have interviewed multiple generations to document traditions and perceptions through time. Eventually, I also plan to interview Hispanics, some of the newest residents of the Upstate, who perform much of the manual labor in the area today. Along with interviews, I have continued participant observation in the crossroads gas stations, at church fish fries, state parks, gated communities, and even at a wilderness bear-hunting expedition.

HISTORICAL SURVEY

The Jocassee Gorges region preserves one of the most beautiful areas in the southeastern U.S. (see Clay 1995, 7). At the very edge of the

Blue Ridge Mountains, cold mountain streams carve gorges through ancient metamorphic rocks and tumble over spectacular waterfalls. Boulder-strewn rivers like the Horsepasture, Whitewater, Keowee, Eastatoee, and Chattooga (the latter comprising much of the setting for the *Deliverance* film) gather together on the Piedmont and flow toward the Atlantic. Deep in the valleys are stands of rhododendron and hemlock, and Oconee bells (one of the world's rarest wildflowers) hide in the shade. Protruding above the trees are occasional outcrops of smooth granitic rock, with sheer sides and romanticized names like "Table Rock" and "Caesar's Head."

Scotch-Irish settlers, traveling southwestward down the edge of the Blue Ridge from Virginia and Pennsylvania, displaced the original Cherokee inhabitants by the late eighteenth century (Clay 1995, 22-23). These highlanders created farms in the valleys, gave their livestock free range through the hills, and transformed much of their corn crop into "runs" of moonshine. Besides the distilling process (and the term "run"), these settlers contributed characteristic words to the area's dialect, such as the aspirated "(h)it," "you-uns" (for you, plural), and the distinctive pronunciations of "chimlee" (chimney), "strenth," and "lenth" (Montgomery 2005). Even today, residents distinguish between "Piedmont" and "mountain" ways of speaking.

Another significant contribution by these mountain residents was the entrenchment of the region's "frontier" reputation. Already on the Cherokee-Charles Town trading frontier, by the early nineteenth century the region had solidified this reputation. Far from the legal centers of major cities and even county seats, people traditionally relied on neighbors for support and settled disputes among themselves. Those living within the law knew better than to report on those living just beyond the edge. Eccentricities of all types were tolerated, and "local characters" abounded in every neighborhood.

After the "War Between the States," freed African Americans settled in small pockets of the Upstate, farming and laboring. Existing
with their white neighbors in an uneasy symbiotic relationship requiring tact and caution, blacks worked in the same fields and often
drank from the same dippers as their white neighbors, yet simultaneously lived in constant fear of harassment and in continual poverty
of resources. Segregated black schools received inadequate funding
and outdated textbooks well into the 1960s. Community residents
recall with vivid terror episodes of white gangs beating black youth,
the afternoon North Carolina Klansmen shot up the neighborhood,
and the night forty years ago the local KKK burned the community's
historic church.

By the early twentieth century, cotton mills had become significant employers in most of the upper Piedmont towns, drawing
mountain folk from the hills and valleys into electrified homes on
paved streets, with better schools and more secure wages (Gauzens
1993, 164; McFall 1959, 146; Clay 1995, 24-25). Eventually, modernization penetrated even the deepest mountain coves, bringing paved
highways, electric lights, refrigerators, radios, televisions, and broadened horizons (Hembree 2003, 110).

Timber companies, another major regional employer, had for
a century extended rails and land purchases into the high country
in an insatiable thirst for lumber (Hembree 2003, 113, 120; Duncan
1984, 4-5; 13). One of those companies, Crescent Land and Timber,
was a subsidiary of Duke Power, a company with an eye for much
greater future development.

Targeting the Keowee River and its tumbling mountain tributar-
ies, in the early sixties Duke began a major push to buy as much
land as possible in order to construct an interconnected series of hy-
droelectric lakes (Badenoch 1989, 17). Eventually the Keowee and
Jocassee valleys were flooded, displacing hundreds of people and

necessitating the destruction of farmsteads, the loss of private land, the removal of churches, and the reburial of ancestors (Lane 2004, 31). Surrendering homes, lands, and history proved to be dishearten- ing to all; but some reaped economic advantages and obtained new- er homes closer to medical and educational institutions (Hembree 2003, 7).

Soon after, Duke re-sold significant portions of the former hill- sides (now lakeshores) to private development companies, who ea- gerly constructed a series of gated and exclusive communities along the lakes. "Snowbirds" from the North and West moved in, bring- ing new accents and new values—but also new tax dollars and new employment opportunities (Badenoch 1989, 37, 62). Within the past several decades, Hispanics have also moved into the Upstate com- munities, bringing a new language, a new religion, and a ready and willing labor force for the construction and landscaping businesses.

Emerging as a lightning rod for the conflicting meanings and uses of physical and social space was McKinney Chapel, in upper Pickens County. Originally on a hillside near the junction of Eastatoee Valley with Jocassee Valley above the Keowee River, the chapel remained a community gathering place for over a century. After the valleys flooded in the 1960s, the country road leading past the church then dead-ended into Lake Keowee just below the dam for Lake Jocassee. For a time, Eastatoee Valley residents could still freely visit McKin- ney Chapel and the cemetery there, as well as boat, picnic, fish, and hike at the lake. By the nineties, however, a private community on the lakeshore restricted lake access, and (after a long court battle) the development company (with governmental approval) gated the public road leading to the chapel. While the developer agreed to al- low permanent public access to the lake, chapel, and cemetery, and the gate guards will wave anyone right through if one mentions an appropriate destination, most Eastatoee Valley residents today refuse to pass through the gates, disdaining having to "beg permission" from outsiders to visit a public place and their ancestors' graves.

DISCUSSION

The key to understanding the passion of people for the region, I believe, lies in unlocking the multilayered meanings of space and place, both geographical and social, embedded here. I have just begun to explore these complex theoretical relationships, also noted (among other places) in the Mississippi Delta of Arkansas by Susan Probasco (2005); the Jocassee Gorges area seems to be another promising case study.

Threaded throughout the narratives and observations I continue to collect are two separate and contrastive themes, providing juxtaposed images of this place, the meanings of this place, and the relationships of those within it. On the one hand, and especially to outsiders, the place is a physical and social frontier with potentially menacing residents (both human and non-human); on the other hand, the place is also majestic, and the residents (including outsiders) deeply committed to this special place. Complicating the analysis, these contrastive themes of place interweave with social relationships, locating individuals within this ambiguous space and through layers of time. In other words, geographical places connect, and are rhetorically connected directly to people (living and dead). Land metaphorically becomes a living being, a critical member of family kinship networks. Likewise, people connect, and are connected to, landscapes—symbolically by means of family stories and actually by means of cemetery burials. For locals, then, losing family land to development equals the death of a family member, and this I believe explains the passion most people have for preserving their family's land. The landscape of the Jocassee Gorges thus becomes a multilayered text of contrastive themes where people and places merge and flow through generations.

The Menacing Frontier

Today, thousands of acres of the Jocassee Gorges region are protected as federal wilderness, National Forest land, the Wild and Scenic Chattooga River, or as state parks. As one travels deeper into the mountain coves, the roads eventually dead-end at isolated trailers or turn into gravel logging roads heading deeper into the back country. Bears routinely raid bird feeders and deer nibble gardens, even in gated communities. A college student remembered "bear scares" cutting their grade-school recess short. In a gated community recently, I have had to wait for deer to cross the road from one fairway to the next.

In thirty years, over thirty people have died trying to run the Chattooga River to emulate the suburbanites in *Deliverance* (Lane 2004, 5). At a local tourist restaurant at the foot of the mountains, T-shirts proclaim: "Keep paddling; I hear banjo music," a joke so deeply embedded in popular culture we still laugh even thirty-five years after the film's premier. James Dickey (1970, 273) described the area as "the Country of Nine-Fingered People and Prepare to Meet Thy God." During the filming of the screenplay, Dickey's son Christopher remembered: "There were plenty of real mountain men out there, with real guns.... I was scared" (1998, 180).

Moonshine (and now illegal drugs) can be easily obtained from the "right" people (see also Hembree 2003, 104). One man I recently interviewed freely admitted that his moonshining activities helped pay for the house he now lived in. Despite having been arrested several times, he stayed in business until a recent injury forced him to retire.

Local residents have told decades-old stories of "quare" folks, including rumors of gay and lesbian couples generally ignored by their religiously conservative neighbors. At a well-known mountain watering hole along a U.S. highway, the former proprietor, "Scatterbrains," once allegedly shot the bar's television to prove he was a faster draw than Sheriff Matt Dillon. "Road Kill Grill," a ramshackle sign currently announces to those driving by. After expressing my curiosity about the bar, I was cautioned by a local woman not to enter the place by myself.

The Majestic Mountains

Simultaneously, the spectacular beauty of the region has fostered in the residents an intimate love affair with the land they occupy. For the locals along the Chattooga, the river "is...something akin to home, a place you feel your connection to very deeply but cannot articulate" (Lane 2004, 18). Debbie Fletcher (2003, 9) described the now-flooded Jocassee Valley as "the nearest place I knew to heaven on earth." As she returns from a trip to her Eastatoee Valley home, Elizabeth Nelson reveals, "my heart jumps when I see that first row of mountains in the distance. It's like, I'm home. Yeah!"

Even those isolated behind the gates of private communities sense this deep-seated association with the land. Overwhelmingly, these residents describe their protected areas as "home," where they feel peace and serenity. Jack Benson and his wife Carol, looking for a place to retire, eventually discovered the flooded valleys in the Upstate: "Lo and behold, here's Lake Keowee," he recalled; "I mean the water is absolutely gorgeous, and the scenery is beautiful countryside." Carol Benson added: "We fell in love with the blue lake."

The Metaphors of Land: Spaces, Places, and Meanings

The meaning of place becomes emotionally intense when one is compelled to surrender that place. Residents forced to move by the rising lake waters somberly told of elderly neighbors who died almost immediately after selling out or who sat on their porch steps one last time as the lake waters lapped inevitably toward the stoop. In two different homes, informants preserve photos of "Chapman's Bridge," a covered bridge originally situated just about where Jocassee Dam looms today. Another man, whose home has been replaced by a state park visitors' center, brought stones from the Whitewater River to line a pathway into his new home's back door. Another resident transplanted rare Oconee bells from Jocassee Valley behind his new home in Eastatoee Valley. In these examples, parts of landscapes (rocks, flowers, bridges) reconnect people to vanished places, and reintegrate those places back into people's lives.

For those who have managed to retain their family lands despite the area's development, those places have transcendent layers of symbolic meanings connecting people into physical and social landscapes. Those who still wander the hills of their youth describe knobs and outcrops and even specific trees in the same intimate detail as an urbanite giving directions to a corner deli. On family farms, granddaughters proudly work the same garden plots alongside their grandmothers, and most high-school students remain close to home after graduation. A young man from northern Pickens County succinctly connects place, time, and social relations as he recalls a recent trip with his father:

> I pointed out a…field that I had picked up hay in, and
> he goes, "well I picked up hay in that same field there,

see, 'cause that used to be your uncle's house across the
street." So I thought that was kind of neat,... doing the
same thing [on the same land] my father had done when
he was younger.

A woman from Eastatoee Valley directly ties herself and her family to her land with spiritual bonds:

I'm the seventh generation of my family to live in this
valley so I have very deep roots here.... If you just go out
and sit and look at it, you can't help but be touched by it
in some fashion. It's a spiritual thing for me. I just feel
like I'm very blessed that I and my family have been allowed to live in this incredible place.

In a wonderful metaphor anthropomorphizing the very terrain
she occupies, Shirley Patterson describes her emotions as she approaches her Upstate home, on land held by her African American
family for over a century. As she tops a hill and sees in the near distance the wall of the Blue Ridge, bookended by the granitic outcrops
of Table Rock and Caesar's Head, she experiences:

...a sense of peace. Peace. You can feel it.... There's something about once I...make that turn right here..., it's just
the serenity and the peace. It's just overpowering. You
can't explain it. You have to feel it.... That whole area just
opens up its arms and just hugs me.

Those born and raised within sight of the Blue Ridge see and feel
a spiritual connection to the place, an intimacy between the land and
the social relationships embedded in those places. "There's a spirit
about this place," Elizabeth Nelson explains; "the day of my dad's funeral,... we started up the road out of the valley and it had the most
empty, spiritless feeling. I'm sure because my dad was gone."

Because of these symbolic and actual familial and generational associations, then, the destruction of these special places because of impounded water or manufactured landscapes creates a sense of personal loss. Land becomes culturally linked to relatives through story and memory and actually linked through burials. Thus, the "death" of the land symbolically means the loss of previous generations and of family memories. Despairing over the flooding of Jocassee Valley, Frank Finley notes that the lake reminds him "of a canopy over a grave" (Hembree 2003, 161), metaphorically associating the death of that landscape with the death of a person. In the Jocassee Gorges region (and probably elsewhere), places become metamorphosed into living beings, and living beings are absorbed back into physical places. This symbolic connection between people and place, I believe, explains the tenacious attempts by locals to protect landscape and thus kinship from destruction.

CONCLUSION

The Jocassee Gorges region is a place of multilayered contrasts of space, place, time, and social relations. Gated community residents love their neighbors but hesitate to shop or dine in nearby local crossroads stores because of the "outsider" glares. Local residents respect the financial contributions of their gated neighbors but resent the new lifestyles locked behind the gates. Both locals and newcomers recognize the "menace" of the mountain frontier, home to bears, moonshiners, and eccentric characters. At the same time, all also recognize the magnificent beauty of the area and the deeply rooted traditional cultures but see those same elements in different ways.

Mountain residents recognize that the place has some negative aspects; but, as with a family member, they accept the faults of the place and love unconditionally. In the Upstate, this love of land equates to a love of family, because land enters the kinship network as another member. More than just the background to events, places connect directly to kin through story, and kin dissolve back into places through time. It is this complicated anthropomorphic metaphor involving a place both menacing and majestic, linked with family and reinforced with spiritual meanings, that explains the multilayered perceptions of the Jocassee Gorges area today.

WORKS CITED

Badenoch, Alice. 1989. *Keowee Key: The Origins of a Community*. Seneca, SC: Jay's Printing Company.

Clay, Butch. 1995. *Chattooga River Sourcebook: A Comprehensive Guide to the River and its Natural and Human History*. [Birmingham, AL]: Chattooga River Publishing.

Dickey, Christopher. 1998. *Summer of Deliverance: A Memoir of Father and Son*. New York: Simon and Schuster.

Dickey, James. 1970. *Deliverance*. Boston: Houghton Mifflin.

Duncan, Dennis, et al, eds. 1984. *An Informal History of Mountain Rest, South Carolina*. Taylors, SC: Faith Printing.

Fletcher, Debbie. 2003. *Whippoorwill Farewell: Jocassee Remembered*. Bloomington, IN: Trafford Publishing.

Gauzens, Joseph. 1993. *Salem: Twice a Town*. Pickens, SC: Hiott Printing.

Hembree, Claudia Whitmire. 2003. *Jocassee Valley*. Pickens, SC: Hiott Printing.

Lane, John. 2004. *Chattooga: Descending into the Myth of Deliverance River*. Athens: University of Georgia Press.

McFall, Pearl Smith. 1959. *It Happened in Pickens County*. Pickens, SC: Sentinel Press.

Montgomery, Michael. 2005. "Voices of My Ancestors: A Personal
        Search for the Language of the Scotch-Irish." *American
        Speech* 80(4): 341-365.

Probasco, Susan. 2005. Unpublished manuscript.

Miss Lillibelle, Moonshine, and Midnight at the Crystal Café: Remembrances of a Southeast Arkansas Culture-Scape

Susan Elizabeth Probasco, University of Arkansas

Driving down Highway 65 South into the extreme southeast Arkansas Delta, eventually you would reach the town of Sweetwater where you might or might not notice a hollowed-out building, worn bricks resting next to a set of defunct railroad tracks. You might notice a deserted ladies' dress shop, an overgrown bottoms area south of town, or fallow fields that were formerly small family homesteads on the periphery of town nestled between curves of the Mississippi River. These are haunted spaces from a town that exists today only in memories. Four sets of narratives collected through the fieldwork process of "visiting" around the Delta transformed the building by the railroad tracks back into the Crystal Café, revisited Lil's Dress Shop where she recalled stories of her favorite days, uncovered the airstrip in the bottoms used by local farmers and merchants where on a hot summer day in 1967 one of the prettiest girls in town became the first woman to fly solo in Chicot County history, and located the family farm where a hapless moonshine runner named Hubert had an unlucky meeting with a couple of revenuers on a Saturday afternoon. Visiting these haunted spaces demonstrates the power of narrative to transform stories of places into remembered spaces and reconfigure an emptying landscape into an immortal topography.

Margaret Jones Bolsterli wrote, "Delta, in this case, means more than topography. It is also a landscape of the mind" (Bolsterli 2000, 1).

Although Bolsterli was speaking more in terms of environmental influence on the Delta psyche, the phrase informed the way I began to see the Delta and to experience that which I could see today, and that which could be reconstructed through stories. Kathleen Stewart's *A Space on the Side of the Road* provides the theoretical basis for recreating spaces on the landscape that today exist only as ruins, or only in memory. Stewart writes of Appalachia as a marginalized South. I would argue that the Delta is marginalized as well, conceived of in the national imagination only in terms of racial strife and demographic insufficiencies. Stewart also writes of Appalachia as a place that is doubly occupied: by the native inhabitants, as well as by the colonial powers of the big businesses that own the land and the mineral rights. Similarly, I would argue also that the Delta is doubly occupied. It is inhabited by its population, the large corporate superfarms that changed the entire social makeup of the region after farm mechanization; and I suggest that it is also occupied with memories of places that exist today only in a "landscape of the mind."

The four narratives that I am presenting are not just excellent examples of taking a moment, as Stewart urges us to do, and sitting to hear a story and re-create a space on the side of the road. The stories also offer poetics of southern womanhood and manhood and use narrative to create a "historic continuity" of place (Bruner 1991, 19-20).

MIDNIGHT AT THE CRYSTAL CAFÉ

Stoddard is an exceedingly handsome man, and he is a very courtly southern gentleman. Every morning at about 4:30 he walks the streets of Sweetwater for exercise. Accompanying him on his walks are two widowed ladies. On his feet are state-of-the-art running shoes sent to him every few months by his son Jay, who participates in Iron Man competitions wherever he travels for business. Stoddard comes well armed, carrying a pistol in his pocket. No danger will befall the ladies while they are with Stoddard. There have been some muggings in town. Stoddard is not taking any chances, nor is he giving up his morning walk. He originally armed himself with an antique revolver, which may or may not have worked, but his sons recently got him a new pistol for Christmas.

Stoddard is from Forrest, Mississippi. In the late 1940s he got out of the Navy, and he went to Jackson, Mississippi, to attend business school. After business school, he got a job as a clerk on a barge in the Mississippi River. The society on the barge was much like the society in the military. There was a captain and other officers. Stoddard sat at the Captain's table and dined with the officers. Stoddard says he thought he was something.

Stoddard was eventually allotted a fine private cabin with his own shower. When he first came onto the barge, Stoddard had to share a cabin equipped with bunk beds with two other men, "and old men at that," he said. One of his roommates drank whiskey and prune juice; and, Stoddard confided in a wry tone, wore silk underwear. After he told me that, he just looked at me, still amused after all these years, and let me absorb the image of a grizzled old river-man swilling whiskey and prune juice, lounging on his bunk in silk underwear. Stoddard's wife Vivian broke the silence by commenting, "How about that!"

One night one of Stoddard's fellow workers asked him if he wanted to go to shore to Sweetwater. Stoddard said, "Sweetwater what?" "Sweetwater, Arkansas," his friend answered; he had a girlfriend there in town. They rode on a tugboat from the barge to a landing on the Arkansas side of the river, and they called a cab to come out to the landing and take them into town. This picture of Sweetwater fascinated me: there have been no taxicabs there in my lifetime, and the little store at the landing has been falling down since I was a child.

When Stoddard and his friend got into town, things were bustling. His friend was to meet his girl at a popular restaurant located next to the train depot. It was open twenty-four hours a day and always busy because of the train traffic. Stoddard remembered, "We walked into the Crystal Grill and Café..." "The Crystal Grill and Café," echoed Vivian, with a smile. Stoddard said simply, "And there was Vivian."

Stoddard was to stay in Sweetwater. Vivian's family was from Sweetwater; in fact, her father owned the Crystal Grill and Café where they met.

I have chosen to present this narrative first because the Crystal Café has completely disappeared from the landscape of Sweetwater. My own mother, a native of Sweetwater, did not know that it had ever existed. Since I was a little girl there had been a hollowed-out building sitting next to the train tracks—no roof, no front, simply piles of bricks, with the ghost of a Dr. Pepper advertisement, advertisement on a wall that was shedding itself in diagonal layers like the sides of a pyramid. Sitting and telling stories with Stoddard and Vivian brought back the years when Sweetwater was a vital town, when the trains brought passengers through, and when young men swam from or took boats from the river barges to the banks of the levee to catch taxis and ride into town in search of pretty girls and fun. Stoddard and Vivian's story re-created this space by the railroad tracks, as well as the cultural space on the edge of the levee where the taxis used to wait for young men who are long gone.

Stewart writes that creating these spaces "begins and ends with the eruption of the local and particular; it emerges in imagination when 'things happen' to interrupt the expected and naturalized, and people find themselves surrounded by place and caught in a haunted doubled epistemology of being in the midst of things and impacted by them and yet making something of things" (1996, 4). I had only ever seen the space as a ruin; never had I imagined it as a magical café, the site of the beginning of a sixty-year romance between Stoddard and Vivian.

Stewart asserts that the spaces on the side of the road "mark the power of stories to re-member things and give them form" (ibid). This power to give the spaces form can be seen in the following narratives as well, whether it is Lil's deserted dress shop, an abandoned air strip, or an abandoned family homestead with naughty secrets.

MISS LILLIBELLE

I have always known Lil as "Aunt Lil." I think that most younger people in town call her Aunt Lil. Her store was open for over forty-five years, far longer than any other business in town except for the beauty shop. The beauty shop has never closed because the owner, Miss Betty Jo, says that no matter what the economy is doing, ladies always want to look pretty. Lil knew everyone in town, as well as everything that was going on. From her spot in the middle of Main Street, just up from City Hall, she could see everything. There was not as much to see as there once was, but she kept up just the same. My mother spent a lot of time at Lil's when she was growing up. Lil's had always been a gathering place, a social place, and that did not change over time. I might have seen any one of a dozen women I knew there any time I dropped by, just sitting on the stools at the back of the store, visiting. Lil used to sit on the counter at the front of the store. There is a spot where the paint is worn away, and the wood is grooved in the shape of a woman's body. The counter tells how she sat in that spot for decades, watching the comings and goings of the town. Several years ago Lil had to have both knees replaced, and she could no longer jump up on the counter. If she was standing next to it, though, her hand would rub back and forth over the spot where the wood is worn so soft, and remember.

One of the last times I went to see Lil I parked across the street from the store. She was sitting at the front, and she saw me before I crossed the street. She said, "Come on in Shug, where you been, watcha doin', where you goin'?" I told her I was coming right there to see her, and she told me to go get myself a "cold co-cola" from the back of the store and then come sit with her behind the counter. We visited for a while. In that time a couple of ladies came in and bought some undergarments, and a couple of other ladies came in and browsed around for a few minutes before leaving empty-handed. As the ladies left, Lil called, "Y'all have a good day and come back," and in the same breath she said, "They can't be from here, I've never seen them in my life."

Lil decided to close early so that she and I could go for a ride around town. I had about an hour until I needed to be back at Stoddard and Vivian's for supper. Riding around in Lil's Cadillac reminded me of when my grandmother still lived in town. Lil used to pick her and my Aunt Sister up at Christmastime and take them for rides to see all of the Christmas lights on the houses around Lake Providence just down across the Louisiana border.

Lil and I rode up and down all of the streets of town. She kept track of the living as well as the dead. She told me where everyone lived and where they used to live, and if there was an empty lot she told me whose house used to be there. We drove by my family's house and both agreed that it didn't look too bad. It did though, and it broke my heart to see it so forlorn and neglected. As we drove back downtown Lil said, "Town's dying, Sugar, I'm going to have to close the shop soon. I can't afford to stay open much longer." I reminded

her that she had said those same words to me almost five years earlier, and she laughed. After our ride Lil dropped me off in town to get
my car and I got back to Stoddard and Vivian's house at five o'clock
on the dot.

Lil was seventy-nine years old and she said, "It's obvious to anyone who looks that I'm no spring chicken." She kept her store because she loved it. Although it was no longer the moneymaker it once
was, the store still served an important function downtown: it was
the anchor. Lil's had always been a gathering place, centrally located
in town as it was, but at that point in the life of the town I think it
was more important that the ladies had somewhere to get together,
in addition to somewhere to buy dresses. Once Lil's closed, the town
lost its symbol of continuity and endurance and, with it, much of its
vitality.

Lil opened her store on Saturday, August 10, 1957; and the town
doctor, Dr. Anderson, came in to look around. Lil started the store
on only $10,000, which she used to buy such things as the display
cases, shoes, and accessories and to advertise. This left precious little
money to buy clothes. Can-can petticoats were the latest style, and
Lil had bought plenty of them and little else. She had them all lined
up around the front of the store, every color of the rainbow, swaying
and bumping against each other like fat colored hens. Dr. Anderson
finished his tour around the store and came up to tell her, "Lillibelle,
you'll never make it." Dr. Anderson is long gone, but Lil's was still
there.

Lil closed the store only on Sundays. In the last few years she and
her husband had moved into town. They used to live outside town on
a large piece of land that had to be mowed with a riding lawn mower
because it was too large to cut with a walking mower. Lil loved to
mow that lawn. She would get up on Sundays and go outside when
it was just getting hot. She would put a Coke in the freezer when she

walked out the door, and when she finished with the yard, the Coke would be partially frozen, enough to be good and slushy. That was her special time, her ritual, and she still dearly missed it.

As she told me that story she ran her hand along the worn groove in the counter where she used to sit and watch all the goings-on in town. The story of the riding lawn mower and the half-frozen Coke, coupled with her unconscious caress of the worn counter, combined in a melancholic moment of loss. Over the course of my research, many women whom I admired and wanted to work with have slipped away, including my sweet grandmother; and now Lil, one of my main informants and the arbiter of all things social in the town, has slipped from her own memories because of Alzheimer's. Her store sits empty on Main Street, except for the bare counters and display cases. The ceiling still shows traces of the pink and gold glitter from the fifties, colors that grew less and less vivid as each year passed.

The story of Lil's shop creates more than a space on the side of the road—it re-creates a space that was the cultural center of town for almost fifty years. The story also offers stories within stories as I serve as the meta-narrator and interpreter, and as Lil "rode" me around town and recreated multiple spaces on the side of the road as she remembered each vacant lot or burned-out building for me. Lil's story also offers a glimpse into a particular southern womanhood of the Arkansas Delta.

Michael Herzfeld (1986) describes those actions which make the Cretan men of Glendi manlier. Herzfeld says that it is not as important to be a good man as to be good at being a man. The enactment of manhood is a form of cultural poetics, and the concept of poetics lends itself as easily to womanhood as it does to manhood. Stoddard embodied all of the aspects that would fulfill the poetics of a certain Delta southern manhood; the women of the Delta have their own poetic. In particular, it involves fulfilling roles traditionally enacted by men and excelling at them while maintaining one's femininity. Both Lil and the pretty girl pilot in the next narrative were experts at this. Lil's husband was from an old farming family, but by the 1980's the viability of the small family farm in the Delta had waned, and Lil kept the family afloat with her business that she ran single-handedly in an efficient and consistent manner for half a century. She found joy in riding a lawn mower on hot Sunday afternoons and anticipating drinking a slushy "co-cola." As she did these things she remained the woman who gowned all the beauty queens and made sure all the ladies looked pretty.

Donna, the pilot, was the product of a man who rivaled the manliness of the tiny Glendiots and a tiny woman who remained fashionable and pretty as she ran the family cement business for forty years. Donna's father did the fieldwork, and her mother ran the business. Although less than five feet tall, Donna's mother ruled big burly men and kept an ivory-handled Colt .45 by her bedside; but she also maintained her 2:00 Friday appointment at the beauty shop for over forty years and collected a legion of size 4 shoes and matching handbags. Donna's parents each embodied a particular poetic of Delta southernness, which combined to form Donna's personal poetics.

THE PRETTY GIRL TAKES FLIGHT

There have been times in her life when Donna has excelled at things that most would consider activities reserved for men. For one thing, Donna can fly. The summer after her freshman year of college, a man was going to teach her older brother Charles to fly. Donna thought she should learn as well. Convincing her daddy was only slightly difficult. This was the man, who, after being questioned by his hunting buddies as to why he was bringing along his little girl to deer camp, for answer slid back the window separating the cab from the bed of the truck, gave Donna his gun where she was sitting with the other men's sons in the back of the truck, and told her to shoot an armadillo that was rooting on the edge of the woods. Donna raised the rifle, took aim, and shot the armadillo clean through. As the armadillo was lifted into the air and flipped by the force of Donna's bullet, the men in the cab of the truck quit talking and said nothing more about her joining future hunting trips.

The fact that her daddy, Harl, would let Donna learn to fly probably didn't surprise many people. He'd been letting her drive around town since she was eleven. But Donna didn't just want to fly. She wanted to fly alone. The fact that Donna would be the first woman to fly a solo flight in Chicot County history did surprise some people. Maybe Harl was finally shaken by something Donna intended to do, for he would not go to the air strip to watch her landing. Instead he had his men at the concrete plant that the family owned lift him up high above the trees in the bucket of a front-end loader so that he could watch from the sky about a quarter mile away from the air strip.

A crowd of men had gathered at the air strip to watch Donna solo that day, including a reporter from the *Memphis Commercial Appeal*. Her older brother, Charles, and their flight instructor, Billy, actually stood out in the middle of the runway. Donna said, "I don't know what they thought they were going to do there." Typically a flight student will land and take off three times in order to pass the solo test. Rather than stop each time, Donna did two touch-and-goes before landing after her third round. This level of skill greatly impressed Billy, and he'll still tell you that Donna was the only student he ever had that would wave at him from the plane as she was making her passes.

Donna so loved flying that her father and another man went in together and bought a plane of their own, a Piper Cub J-3. This is one of the most elementary flying machines, with an extra long wingspan that allows it to act more like a glider than most planes. Donna and Billy had a good time in that plane, landing in unusual places, such as the levee or on a sandbar in the Mississippi River. They practiced stalls and tried to dip the wings into the Grand Lake. Had Harl known any of this, he would have lived in the bucket of the front-end loader.

Driving around town when she was only eleven years old, twirling and tossing flaming batons in high school, racing her Plymouth Barracuda against boys on the straights of Highway 65 South, and finally learning to fly, but then *playing* in the air by stalling and dipping her wings in the river and landing on sandbars—none of these things was quite rational, but the fact that she did them, looking like an angel, only added to Donna's appeal. She continues to embody a particularly striking example of southern womanhood.

THE UNFORTUNATE HUBERT AND THE MOONSHINE

Despite the strong presence of evangelical Protestantism in the region, the Delta historically has been a hotbed of bootlegging activity. According to Willard Gatewood (1993), once the temperance forces in America succeeded in enacting prohibition early in the twentieth century, the answer to the legal ban on alcoholic beverages was a proliferation of bootleggers who supplied large numbers of unlicensed saloons with liquor. In the Delta, these saloons were known as "blind tigers." Throughout Prohibition, the Delta remained a stronghold of opposition to temperance forces in Arkansas. Today, much of Arkansas, governed by staunch conservatives, is "dry," meaning no liquor can be sold legally within the borders of the dry counties. Many of the "wet" counties in the state today are in the Delta.

Much of the liquor consumed in the Delta was homemade. One interesting facet of Delta whiskey production is that the underground industry stayed in business long after Prohibition had been repealed (Hubbell 1993). According to Hubbell, whiskey-making in the Delta was at its peak in the 1930s. Prohibition was repealed in 1933 (Clark 2003), but according to Stoddard, making and selling whiskey in the Delta went on until the outbreak of World War II, when other types of jobs became available. Apparently, bootlegging provided employment in a region where money was tough to come by.

Only recently I learned that my family had a part in this history. Stoddard told me a story, which he said was told to him by my own granddaddy. It seems that Pa Barnes, who was my grandmother's father, was a whiskey producer with another townsman; and, along with some other men from the community, they employed Pa Barnes's sons-in-law to deliver whiskey for them. It was something of a family affair.

Apparently my own granddaddy had a model B Ford, customized for his bootlegging enterprise. In the trunk he kept a fifty-gallon drum and a siphon. He told Stoddard that he used to make whiskey deliveries for Pa Barnes all over the Delta. He would pull up and people would tell them how many gallons they wanted, and that's what he siphoned out. He and my grandmother married in 1935, so he would have started this enterprise well after the repeal of Prohibition.

According to Stoddard and Vivian, whiskey-making was a common occupation in the Delta, and the practice did not reflect badly on the practitioners. Lots of people did it, they told me. When Vivian was a child, her family lived out on the Boeff River (pronounced Beff). She said that she could remember seeing everybody's stills set up out in the slough. (A slough is formed when an oxbow lake becomes so choked up with cypress, lotus, and tupelo trees that there is very little open water left, and the lake is reduced to a narrow channel [Foti 1993]).

However, the fact that many people manufactured and sold whiskey did not make it legal, and occasionally there were consequences. Much of the Barnes family liquor was buried in drums in the potato patch. The men would take long steel rods and probe the ground until they found a drum and then dig it up. One day all the men were going into town except for Hubert, who was the brother of one of the sons-in-law. They all told Hubert, "Don't sell anything while we're gone." Later that afternoon two really "slick looking fellows" came to call. They were dressed up to go out on the town, including fancy straw hats. They said to Hubert, "We hear y'all make the finest whiskey around." Hubert said, "Yeah, I expect we do." They asked if he had any to sell, and he said, "No, not today." The men seemed disappointed and they said, "Well now, that's a real shame because we were looking to buy twenty gallons." Apparently this was a very good sale and Hubert could not bring himself to ignore such a boon. So he grabbed a rod and started probing the potato patch. When he dug a drum of whiskey out of the ground, he was promptly arrested by those two slick fellows. It was not a good day for Hubert.

REMEMBERING THE DELTA

Remembering is a process of creating. Sitting together, visiting, and storytelling facilitate the process of re-creating spaces lost in time. Stopping by seemingly empty spaces on the side of the road and telling stories about them ensures that the exploits of Stoddard and Vivian, Lil, Donna, and Hubert are remembered, and that the haunted and empty spaces of Sweetwater are repopulated and made into what I call an immortal topography. Bolsterli's landscape of the mind becomes immortal through narrative. Stewart described narrative as creating the possibility for alternative realities, creating spaces where things are remembered and given form, spaces where the Othered regions of America find a voice (1996, 4).

Jerome Bruner describes reality as "how we get a reliable fix on the world" (1991, 1). Bruner states that we organize our experiences and memories into narratives and that "narratives, then, are a version of reality whose acceptability is governed by convention and 'narrative necessity' rather than by empirical verification and logical requiredness, although ironically we have no compunction about calling stories true or false" (1991, 5). All of the stories presented here are forms of the truth, the truth as my informants would have me know it, reality as they would have it remembered. Bruner suggests that the narrative form is the best mechanism for gleaning how reality is represented in the act of knowing. He states that "what creates a culture, surely, must be a 'local' capacity for accruing stories of happenings of the past into some sort of diachronic structure that permits a continuity into the present—in short, to construct a history, a tradition, a legal system, instruments assuring historical continuity if not legitimacy" (1991, 19-20). The Delta narratives not only create spaces on the side of the road in which forms of reality can be re-created and remembered, but also highlight the poetics of Delta southernness. As such, they exemplify Bruner's local capacity of turning stories of the past into history through narrative.

WORKS CITED

Bolsterli, Margaret Jones. 2000. *Born in the Delta: Reflections on the Making of a Southern White Sensibility*. Fayetteville: University of Arkansas Press.

Bruner, Jerome. 1991. "The Narrative Construction of Reality." *Critical Inquiry* 18(1)1-21.

Clark, Norman H. 2003. "Prohibition (U.S. History)." *Microsoft Encarta Online Encyclopedia*. http://encarta.msn.com.

Foti, Thomas. 1993. "The River's Gifts and Curses." In *The Arkansas Delta: Land of Paradox*, edited by Jeanne Whayne and Willard B. Gatewood, 30-57. Fayetteville: University of Arkansas Press.

Gatewood, Willard B. 1993. "The Arkansas Delta: The Deepest of the Deep South." In *The Arkansas Delta: Land of Paradox*, edited by Jeanne Whayne and Willard B. Gatewood, 3-29. Fayetteville: University of Arkansas Press.

Herzfeld, Michael. 1986. "The Poetics of Manhood." In *Poetics of Manhood: Contest and Identity in a Cretan Mountain Village*, 3-50. Princeton: Princeton University Press.

Hubbell, Kenneth R. 1993. "Always a Simple Feast: Social Life in the Delta." In *The Arkansas Delta: Land of Paradox,* edited by Jeanne Whayne and Willard B. Gatewood, 184-207. Fayetteville: University of Arkansas Press.

Stewart, Kathleen. 1996. *A Space on the Side of the Road: Cultural Poetics in an Other America.* Princeton: Princeton University Press.

Objects of Desire: Photographs and Retrospective Narratives of Fieldwork in Indonesia

Jennifer W. Nourse, University of Richmond

This discussion of my fieldwork, memory, and experience begins with a nod to Handler and Gable's essay (this volume) in which they ask what anthropology can contribute to the study of social memory. I take Gable and Handler's insights about the false dichotomy between memory and history (since, they argue, all history and memory are perspectival) and consider ways in which fieldwork photographs demonstrate the same point. I suggest that my photographs became the repositories for individual interpretations of a host of broader issues related to the nation-state and its agenda. This agenda was reflected in ways the photographs were framed, exchanged, and narrated by anthropologists/photographers and recipients of the photographs as presentations.

In Sulawesi, Indonesia, where I have conducted intermittent but intensive fieldwork since the 1980s, I found that the photos I had taken could act as objects that froze my own and others' memories of the past to events depicted within the borders of the pictures. In other contexts, they were like social contracts, binding present relationships to past in a more fluid and encompassing manner. Both the Indonesians who received the photos as gifts and I who had not seen them since the 1980s were unaware that the ways in which we had posed, stored, or narrated the photos were inflected by broader political and economic forces. Now, cognizant of the impact such forces have had on both my fieldwork and perception of self and others, I am concomitantly conscious that all memory is perspectival and presentistic. My conclusions, thus, coincide with Gable and Handler's.

THE "OLD" PERSPECTIVE OF FIELDWORK: NOT SEEING THE STATE

These insights surfaced when, in preparation for a PowerPoint retrospective presentation on fieldwork for the Southern Anthropological Society meetings of 2008, I began to digitize negatives and slides that I had not seen since they were taken in the 1980s. From 1984-1986 I conducted fieldwork among so-called tribal people in upland Sulawesi, Indonesia, where I photographed myriad scenes and people. From my 21st-century perspective, it became clear that many of the photos taken had been unwittingly choreographed with categories delineating who was "modern" and who was not—categories that had been promulgated by the Indonesian state during the Suharto regime (1966-1998). Though I had consciously rejected as offensive the claims of the Suharto government that uplanders like the Lauje I studied were inferior to the modern lowlanders, because of their more "primitive subsistence [swidden] agriculture," I nevertheless regarded the lowlanders, as the Indonesian bureaucracy did, as "modern." Following the Indonesian state's contention that its bureaucrats and educated middle class who lived in coastal towns throughout Indonesia were the most civilized and "modern" group of citizens, I did not realize that these state categories had preconditioned me to regard the superficial trappings of "modernity" such as tennis clothes and kids on bicycles as so similar to my own experiences that there was no question that Tinombo dwellers were indeed "modern" like me and, therefore, "different" from the highlanders. It was only after

I scanned negatives I had not seen in 25 years that the pictures of the young "moderns" in Tinombo seemed quaint, provincial, and not as distinct from the upland photos as I had originally thought.

For the first three months of my fieldwork, I lived in the coastal, "modern" town of Tinombo, with my new husband, "Mr. Eric." There we learned the upland language, Lauje, and waited for the flooded rivers to subside so we could hike to the highlands and begin "real" fieldwork. Anxious to meet as many people as possible, Mr. Eric and I accepted all invitations, using the occasions as a chance to learn the mechanics of our new camera by taking photos and offering them as gifts (*prestasi*) to the subjects. In almost all of these contexts, one or the other of us was usually asked to pose next to a "modern" Tinomboan. For instance, recently digitized images revealed a "holiday piknik" taken in 1984 at a nearby waterfall with young Tinombo bureaucrats and merchants. I now see the Ray-Bans, swimming suits, and Nike running shoes as conspicuous items to mark these people as affluent and stylishly "modern," and I wonder if Mr. Eric and I were not one more status marker when we were included in the photos of moderns.

Most of the digitized negatives revealed photo after photo of Tinombo's brides and grooms with either Mr. Eric, me, or both of us posing next to the bride and groom. These photos made us known throughout Tinombo; we quickly became "hot commodities"; every newlywed couple in Tinombo wanted their picture taken with us in the second, *modern*, phase of the ceremony. (See figure 10.1.)

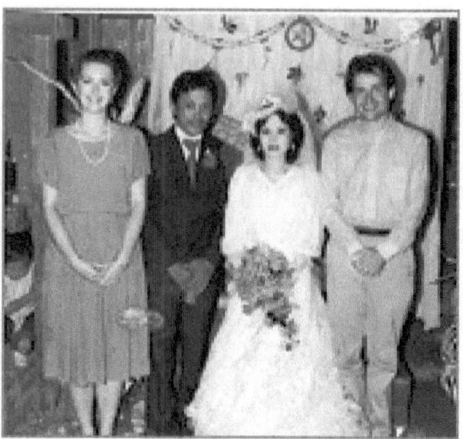

Figure 10.1. Wedding in Tinombo in 1984.

The first phase consisted of the bride and groom, dressed in full co-lonial regalia, the indigenous (*asli*) segment of the ceremony, posi-tioned on stage in front of the audience. At the end of the wedding, during the modern segment, the couple changed into full western garb, the bride in white gown and the groom in suit and tie. Here, while a rock band played Beatles music, Mr. Eric and I were asked to pose with the couple while someone else took pictures using our camera. The photos we developed became our wedding gift, includ-ing a framed 5 x 7 print of us with the bride and groom. We were often surprised later to find these photos displayed on a wall in the newlyweds' front parlor. The requisite pose with the bride in white wedding dress and face powdered until it was pale white did not seem odd until I reviewed the digital images recently, 25 years after the fact, and juxtaposed them with upland wedding pictures.

There are fewer upland wedding photos in my collection, and Mr. Eric and I were never asked to pose with newlyweds nor with their families for photos. At first glance, uplanders appear more tradi-tional than modern lowlanders. For instance, an upland bride and groom never changed clothing, remaining in traditional sarong and headdress throughout the ceremony. At the time I thought that the uplanders' consistently traditional clothing indicated that they were less acculturated to "modernity." Now, however, I see more similarity than difference between uplanders and lowlanders. In every upland wedding sequence, at least one wedding photo incorporated a shot of the bride and groom beneath President Suharto's picture. No matter how poor the family was, they displayed a photo (perhaps unframed if truly poor) of the President on the wall of their bamboo hut in what could be loosely termed the "front parlor." (See Figure 10.2.)

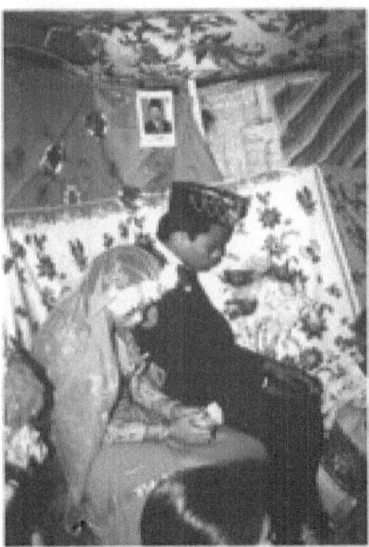

Figure 10.2. Taipaobal Wedding Couple with Suharto Picture in Background

In wedding portraits, whether the President's face was included inadvertently (a distinct possibility) or purposely choreographed by members of the wedding, the iconic face of Suharto, representing the coercive "New Order" regime, revealed how deeply the state's tentacles had reached upland communities. Despite the fact that the Suharto government had categorized these people as *suku terasing*, as non-citizen tribals, these upland Lauje regarded themselves as national citizen-subjects and made that claim by hanging the President's photo on the wall and by asking a government representative, the lowland mayor, to speak at their weddings. They did just as lowlanders did.

The presence of Suharto's Mona Lisa-like smile in upland wedding photos and the young and earnest anthropologists in lowland images suggests that both uplanders and lowlanders are making similar statements by referring to the state. Suharto's New Order regime concertedly strove to "modernize" Indonesia through massive (World Bank-sponsored) social engineering projects. Giant billboards and TV commercials advertised Suharto's family planning program (the central component in his scheme) with smiling faces of a Eurasian-looking couple and their two westernized children, urging: "Come On! Let's Modernize!" "A Small Family is a Happy Family."

Although his face did not appear in the wedding photos of lowlanders, Suharto's influence did. Lowlanders made themselves look like the westerners from Suharto-era billboards, whether in clothing, in lightened (powdered) faces, or through requests that western anthropologists stand beside them. For Lowlanders, all things western became synecdoches for all things modern as well as all things nationally sanctioned by the state as exclusive objects for ideal citizens. Thus the tennis outfits and rock bands made lowlanders appear to be more modern than uplanders, whom the state defined as "foreign tribes" (*suku terasing*), lower in rank than lowland citizens. Uplanders, unaware that the state regarded them as beyond development, too primitive to climb the ranks of an evolutionary ladder that would eventually lead to civilization, mimed the actions of lowland moderns by placing Suharto's photo in prominent places in their homes and asking bureaucrats to speak at their weddings. In the process they revealed a desire to be recognized as citizen-subjects, a desire just as intense as that of the lowlanders. The photos of both lowlanders and uplanders conveyed the same message, but lowland photos including westerners like Mr. Eric and me revealed an awareness that embodying things western signified their loyalty to the state's development agenda. Simultaneously, these prominently displayed photos with westerners marked the owners and the household dwellers as well-positioned citizens at the apex of a state imposed hierarchy of status and privilege that excluded those defined as foreign tribes.

When I returned to the field in 1997, right before Suharto was deposed and after my own eleven-year absence, and now with two children as well as Mr. Eric, these hierarchies were more clearly drawn; Suharto's modernization and development policies had allowed those at the apex of the hierarchy to prosper and those at the bottom to sink even lower. In lowland Tinombo, the number of satellite dishes, new motorcycles, and houses equipped with electricity was astounding. Tinombo streets were now rather empty in the early evening as the gray glow of TV screens kept the family members of the modern merchant class indoors watching *Baywatch* or *MTV-Asia*. If I did encounter a young person on the street, usually from a poorer foothills family without a TV, instead of politely greeting me as they had in the past, or asking the usual set of questions about where I was from and what birth control I used, they would look at me and say in English (not understood at all prior to this), "Hello, Mrs. I Fuck You." Now this may have been a mistranslation of the 1980s greeting, "Hello, Mister (in English) I Love You." Nevertheless, this new statement was off-putting, to say the least.

Even merchant class youth resented the western lifestyle Suharto had recommended that everyone embrace, for it was not as readily available as the regime had promised. Though still desiring contact with westerners, the resentment seethed beneath the surface. Rather than directly confront me or Mr. Eric, though, some of that resentment was deflected to our two children, Larsen, 7 years old, and Grace, almost 2. Requests for photos with them, especially in retrospect, verged on the scary. Hundreds of strangers wanted pictures with Grace and they would even try to grab her out of our arms. Grace was at the most adorable age as far as Indonesians were concerned, and she had the most desirable hair color, blonde. Strangers of all kinds, travelling through town on the Trans-Sulawesi highway, in buses or jeeps, and stopping for a restaurant break in Tinombo, would see me or Mr. Eric with Grace and rush toward us, begging for posed pictures. Now, though, people had their own cameras and they shot photos even as we walked away to protect exhausted Grace from the disconcerting flashbulbs. Many people came to pinch Grace's cheek, especially pregnant women; they believed touching the cheek of a European child while one was pregnant would bestow lighter-colored skin and prosperity on the prospective newborn. But these women pinched her hard! Grace became so used to aggressive squeezing that when a stranger neared her she began wildly swinging her arms and yelling guttural defensive gibberish.

At this time, overt aggression toward the West had intensified generally. Demonstrations in Jakarta called for multinational companies to divest from Indonesia until Suharto was ousted. Average Indonesians were well aware the Suharto family had accepted bribes from American businessmen representing oil and other multinational corporations so they could conduct business in Indonesia. Suharto had embezzled $15-35 billion dollars—$12 billion of which was inaccessibly stashed in an Austrian bank, while the rest of the country remained impoverished (BBC News 2004). The fact that average Indonesians were antagonistically pinching Grace's cheeks while superficially interacting in a friendly manner revealed resentment over their perceived lack of economic advancement vis-à-vis Westerners. Acting politely (*halus*) on the surface, while feeling turmoil (*kasar*) internally, was a key behavior of civilized elites that Geertz had repeatedly described (1976; 1981). Knowing what Geertz said, however, did not help our surprise at the duplicitous pinches. We often responded by running, Grace snuggled in a backpack until we could duck into a friend's house to escape. When explaining the chase to our modern friends, the initial panic eventually abated. One woman laughingly said it reminded her of the Beatles' movie *Help!* Her comment reframed Grace (and us) into rock stars and the raw fear (a *kasar* emotion) into a more honed (*halus*) recognition that we were an elite group in the eyes of locals.

Larsen's experience, at least initially, did not instill the same degree of panic. He was invited to a series of birthday parties at the homes of *nouveau-riche* Tinombo children. All the children, dressed in their finest, wore themed birthday party hats, ate boxed lunches, drank from matching themed party cups (Pokeman or Star Wars), and dabbed their mouths with matching napkins. The scenes were vaguely reminiscent of an American birthday party. But there were differences; approximately fifty 6-8 year olds sat perfectly still in chairs carefully placed in a circle around the birthday child's living room, while listening quietly as Tinombo's elementary school principal spoke about the importance of schooling for "national progress and modernity." Larsen would be asked to stand next to the birthday child for the "cutting of the cake photo." Candles were lit, never to be blown out, while the birthday child stood on one side, holding a knife, pretending to cut the cake, and Larsen stood on the other side, smiling. The photos looked like exact replicas of what might be shown on American TV, but the actions and meaning behind the images were quite different. The presence of the state (in the school principal), the fact that the children were so still and quiet, and the fact that the birthday cake was neither cut nor shared made me realize that people here may look like westerners, but the meaning they derived from their behavior was much closer to what locals in the uplands were thinking and doing. Both sets of acquaintances wanted to demonstrate they were loyal citizens of Suharto's westernized state, but not all had the means to do so. Those who could, claimed their place at the apex of the Suharto hierarchy by miming all things western, but resentment toward Suharto and westerners seethed just beneath the smiling faces of these model citizens.

That these were merely "pretend" American birthday parties was clear to 7-year-old Larsen, who complained, "Parties here are no fun 'cause all we do is sit still and we don't even get to eat the cake!" To appease Larsen I bought him and another boy, Iki, bicycles and squirt guns. While I conducted interviews with midwives and clinic personnel in Tinombo, Larsen and his friend rode through the town chasing the pedicab (*becak*) drivers and squirting them with water guns. I had heard a few people tell me Larsen should be more careful. In retrospect, I think they disapproved of his energy and freedom of movement, but in typical Indonesian fashion they never said so directly. Within a week, Iki's father had taken away his son's bicycle, saying, "Iki is too naughty." I ignored this cultural cue, intent instead on pleasing Larsen. One day, Larsen, now the lone bicyclist, rushed out to squirt the young tough guy peddling the pedicab without a passenger. Before Larsen had a chance to squirt him, the fellow kickboxed Larsen in the chest, knocked him off his bike into an open sewerage canal, and spat on him. Larsen, scratched, bleeding, and scared, returned home crying. Most adults commiserated, but two of my close friends told me that "Larsen got what he deserved; he should not have been chasing a driver while he was working." Another said, "It's not right for a well-brought-up lad like Larsen to behave like a young street urchin who is uncivilized."

I realized I had mistakenly allowed Larsen to act in a way that allied him with lower-class pedicab drivers. The "moderns" in Tinombo believed Larsen deserved the treatment he received. Nevertheless, these same "moderns," all elites in the community, people who had shared "pikniks" to waterfalls with me and Mr. Eric years before, or had hung wedding photos with me and Mr. Eric in them on their parlor wall, had, unbeknownst to me, called an impromptu town meeting in which they asked the mayor to see that the angry pedicab driver was reprimanded. The hierarchy of position, power, and citizenship was clearly evident here. No wonder the lower-status pedicab driver took out his resentment toward elites and foreigners on an American child. In these months right before Suharto was ousted from office, most coastal dwellers, of any class or status, knew that none of the American oil company executives who had bribed Suharto and his cronies was being questioned for his actions. There was talk among Tinombo people loyal to Suharto and his family that Suharto was not completely at fault, for the corruption had involved westerners as well as him. As one Tinombo man said to me about the Suharto crisis, "A bribe passes between two hands, yet here only one hand is being blamed or being caught." Larsen and I were receiving privileged treatment, even though we had defied local standards of propriety. Despite their inner resentment, elites smoothed over or made refined (*halus*) their rough feelings about our inappropriate conduct.

Revisiting these incidents recalled by photos provides a new perspective on civilized behavior, modernity, globalization, and the state. For Indonesian "moderns" who worked for the Suharto bureaucracy, the world was structured in the same way as it had been during colonial times; the world was conceived in terms of a Lewis Henry Morgan-style hierarchy with its Social Darwinist overtones (Duncan, 2004). "Modern" people regarded themselves as more refined (*halus*) and therefore civilized because they smoothed things over, made the rough and negative seem positive. The less civilized, the crude ones (*kasar*), revealed their inner emotions and struggles; they moved, sweated, and toiled in the fields (or on pedicabs) in a system that placed the effortless, seemingly refined activity of bureaucrats and merchants on the highest rungs of a ladder and the sweaty, toiling, angry actions of farmers or pedicab drivers on the lowest rungs. When I let Larsen act like a "worker," I also revealed the sham of the effortless western-life of prosperity that was the promised reward for all those "modern" Suharto bureaucrats. Suharto's state had promised that if Indonesians behaved as if they were "modern" and western, if they had smaller families, and if they looked as if they lived effortless lives, then they eventually would have those lives. The modern bureaucrats had allied themselves with me and my family in the 1980s because they desired the refined status that we represented. In the earlier photos in which Mr. Eric or I were included with the elites, the inclusion marked them as if they were on the same rung of the civilization ladder as Americans. The moderns' wedding photos did not merely signify a desire to be like westerners, it marked the people in the images as superior to anyone else in the community and equal to elites throughout Indonesia and beyond.

At this moment, though, the year before Suharto's regime finally fell, the prosperity that his New Order regime had promised had not materialized for everyone. At the end of the 1990s, the happiness that was tantalizingly revealed through images of prosperity in TV programs beamed from Jakarta or in American TV programs was now revealed as a false promise, never to be attained for the average Indonesian. The Tinomboers who had educated themselves, married later, and practiced family planning, just as the government had urged, regarded the pledged rewards from association with the West to be, in reality, a sham. Tinomboers who had not known me or Mr.

Eric during the past, and with whom we had no prior social relationship, reacted as one would to anyone seeming to represent the
broken promises of Suharto's scheme; they reacted with contempt
(the spitting and the comments) and brutality (kickboxing a 7-year-
old child). Still unable to critique their government, the resentment
erupted against Westerners like me and my children because the coercive Suharto regime prohibited dissension. When young men ut-
tered, "Hello, Mrs. I Fuck You," the phrase contained multiple sub-
texts of significance.

HOW I BECAME A BLONDE: MIMING FOR THE STATE

By 2001, Indonesia had elected two Presidents since Suharto left office and was adjusting to democracy, transparent government, and
free markets. Beleaguered by the Asian financial crisis and clear evidence of corruption in his cabinet, the Indonesian Senate (MPR) in a
special session impeached President Wahid in July 2001 and elected
Megawati Sukarno as President. Sulawesians talked of her creden-
tials as a businesswoman and claimed, falsely, that she had attended
Georgetown with Bill Clinton and their friendship would thus improve Indonesian business. Meanwhile President Wahid refused to
relinquish power to Megawati. The nation was paralyzed. In transit
to Tinombo, I was stuck in a Best Western hotel in South Sulawesi
when all airports, government offices, and banks shut down. It was
days before I could reach Tinombo. Contacting friends I knew in
this town, I arranged to meet at one of the few open places in Makas-
sar, the Yuppi salon. Lili told me, "Salons are always open in a crisis
because the stylists give the gift (*prestasi*) of making everyone look
refined (*halus*) on the outside. Just like they do at weddings. If we feel
rough or crude (*kasar*) on the inside, the stylists make us seem refined and soon we feel like we look." The exchange rate being favorable to me, I offered to treat my friends to a cut and style. I decided

on blonde highlights. As stylists combed and coiffed, we all talked, revealing our inner fears; some worried about demonstrations and riots, others feared their marooned husbands/partners would stray. I spoke about my impending divorce. To soothe us, two male stylists dressed in wigs, gowns, and heels began to sing "I Will Survive" and other '70s and '80s feminist pop songs. The blonde highlighting solution, left on my hair longer than it should have been during the cabaret show, resulted in a new overall haircolor—blonde. One friend exclaimed, "Isn't it wonderful? You forgot about your own problems, we about our country's problems, and now you look like a real Western woman. You have blonde hair."

When I arrived ten days later in Tinombo, my friends told me, "You look like the deceased Princess Diana." When I asked them to explain what they meant, one friend said, "Now you are a more appropriate and better Western female." In the foothills towns of Dusunan and Lombok, many people just stared at me, rather than enthusiastically greet me as before. They retrieved photos of me from 17 years earlier. It was clear that my brown hair from the past and blonde coiffure in the present confused them. One man said, "See this picture, remember? Mr. Eric took this picture with you, me, and my grandmother. You look different now, but you are the same person, aren't you? You do remember?" Over the first few days I was there, incidents like these happened repeatedly. Eventually, subtly, after telling me about what had happened to all the others in the photo, the presenter of the photo would say something like "Remember how my grandmother told you secrets and showed you the ritual for healing malaria? You brought sugar and cooking oil to my grandmother." I recognized they were too proud to directly ask for money or goods, and they were jogging my memory so I would recall my past debts and obligations and respond appropriately. The photograph was a material reference to my prior gift and proof of our relationship. As a social contract reminding me to continue acting as an ideal citizen, the photo prompted me to give a gift in a refined way, not crude nor embarrassing.

Later that same evening, I brought some photos of one of the midwives of her now-deceased grandmother, an image Si Giombang had asked for when I had visited the year before. She had been reluctant then to answer my new research questions about midwifery and the government, and I think my frustration had shown. I had not been able to tell if she had frozen my research questions into her memory of the past when I was more interested in ritual secrets, which she willingly proffered, or if she was hiding her negative opinions about the government's women's health programs. She said, "My grandmother told me long ago she was willing to reveal secrets to you because you had come to the village like good Lauje spirits come, as a husband-wife pair." Tears welled up in my eyes. I explained I was in the middle of a divorce. She confessed she was having identical husband problems. We eventually turned to the positive and discussed the wonderful children we had had from these husbands. Suddenly I realized, in the process of talking, Si Giombang had now answered the questions I had asked the year before.

The photos and memories we had exchanged were the gifts we gave to each other to recollect the happier moments of our lives and smooth over the rough ones. Si Giombang had been hesitant the year before to talk about the government health clinic and her dismay at its condescending attitude to midwives such as herself. Perhaps this was because it might indicate that she did not belong to the national community of good citizens. As a foothills Lauje woman who was constantly regarded by "moderns" in Tinombo as one step away from a *suku terasing* or primitive tribal person (especially since she practiced "traditional" medicine and believed in placental spirits [Nourse 1999]), she avoided criticizing the government to my face.

This exchange brought our relationship back to the state of inter-action that the government elites, even in post-Suharto times, ad-mired; the interaction now was that between proper citizens who "foster social connectivity" through gift exchange (Boellstorf 2007, 67; Pemberton 1994, 9).

CONCLUSION: WHICH NATIVES' POINT OF VIEW?

The "gift," *prestasi* in Indonesian, a loan word from Dutch, had be-come a central feature of Suharto era designations of good citizen-ship and, inadvertently, a component of my gifts of photographs in the 1980s. For lowlanders in Tinombo, or in the foothills, my photos represented a situated social relationship, an exchange in which the photo itself, as a gift, acted as a social contract, evoking perhaps tacit, perhaps overt, Works Cited to national belonging. The photos served as an icebreaker for recalling a host of relationships in and out of the picture's frame. In post-Suharto times, people brought these pho-tos out because, newly blonde, I no longer looked like the person in the photo. Moreover, the urgency, even desperation, with which they presented them revealed that the photos represented more than just a memory of a moment. These images had become tickets to national belonging and social and moral responsibility, an obligation to re-ciprocate, to exchange friendship and empathy for information, per-spective, and occasional provisions. The memories evoked by these photos, at once disembodied from the blonde I now was and the bru-nette I had been, were no longer unmoored from a narrative having to do with a transformation to someone else that was brought about by Indonesians trying to help me be the best Westerner I possibly could be. In some senses, then, as a blonde, I had become more like them; performing as the Tinombo moderns dressed in white wed-ding gowns and powdered faces were, as the iconic Western female. I now posed like the blonde princess they saw on TV, though they knew she was dead and I was brunette. They knew they too were not authentic Westerners, but we all feigned happiness, pretended to be ideal citizen-subjects, while also knowing that beneath the smiles, peroxide and powder were secrets, lies, and struggles. Something in the act of doing the performing brought out the similarities and differences between us all. Both of us were shaped by the personal as well as the political.

In conclusion, I support Gable and Handler's point that memory, whether theirs or ours, is recollected through a perspectival and presentistic lens. I suggest, then, that if a "native point of view" about memory exists, as Gable and Handler suggest, it is one that is dialogic, shaped in interaction with an anthropologist and mediated by his or her recollected and theoretical perspective about what authentic worldviews are. Ethnographies and recollections of fieldwork rarely reveal an authentic native voice but are mediated through an anthropologist who translates into English what authentic natives believe. Both "the native" and "the anthropological" perspectives are layered perspectival descriptions reflecting multiple social and temporal interpretations of the past as the present shifts. Thus photos do not reveal the facts of experience any more than memories do, and neither do the narratives about them. What photos can reveal is that the images of self and other embedded in one's memories are inflected by categories of sameness and difference prevalent at a particular point in time and shaped by more hegemonic state and/or disciplinary agendas. Culture and memory are neither frozen nor hegemonic recitations of an authentic past, nor mere individual perspectives, but continually negotiated dialogues reflecting the elusive and shifting boundaries dividing "natives views of us" and "ours of them."

WORKS CITED

BBC World News Online. 2004. Suharto Tops Corruption Rankings. Thursday, March 25. http://news.bbc.co.uk/go/pr/fr/-/2/hi/ business/3567745.stm.

Boellstorf, Thomas. 2007. *A Coincidence of Desires: Anthropology, Queer Studies, Indonesia*. Durham, NC: Duke University Press.

Duncan, Christopher. 2004. *Civilizing the Margins: Southeast Asian Government Policies for the Development of Minorities*. Ithaca: Cornell University Press.

Gable, Eric, and Richard Handler. 2008. "Forget Culture, Remember Memory?" Keynote Address. March 15. Southern Anthropological Society Meetings, Staunton, Virginia.

Geertz, Clifford. 1976. *Religion of Java*. Chicago: University of Chicago Press.

———. 1981. Negara: *The Theater State in Nineteenth Century Bali*. Princeton, NJ: Princeton University Press.

Nourse, Jennifer. 1999. *Conceiving Spirits: Birth Rituals and Contested Identities among Lauje of Indonesia*. Washington, DC: Smithsonian Institution Press.

Pemberton, John. 2004. *On the Subject of Java*. Ithaca, NY: Cornell University Press.

Memory and Celebration in Contemporary San Miguel de Allende, Mexico

Samantha Krause, Florida State University

San Miguel de Allende is an historic city in Guanajuato, Mexico. It is a relatively small city, with a population of about 80,000 in the urban area, located about four hours north of Mexico City. Since the 1960s, the city has become a hub of activity for foreigners and tourists. It advertises itself as an attractive retirement destination for American and Canadian retirees, and thus it has an influential *gringo* population. In many of the city's central areas, English is spoken just as much as Spanish. Phone booths advertise low rates for those phoning "home" to North America, and the public library offers English and Spanish novels in equal numbers. This melding of cultures is striking, and it makes San Miguel an excellent venue in which to observe the concepts of memory and identity, both for the immigrant *gringos* and the native Mexican populations.

The idea that immigration transforms and shapes a culture is basically universal. When two or more groups of people of differing cultures coexist in one area, the two groups will adapt to whichever aspects of the other foreign culture they find the most beneficial. Marshall Sahlins expands on these concepts of exchange in his research on the contact period of the Hawaiian Islands (1981). The migration pattern of American citizens moving to Latin America, although not as much studied as Latin American immigration to the United States, has nevertheless given rise to the term "reverse immigration" in response to this phenomenon. Novels such as *Fall-ing...in love with San Miguel* and *On Mexican Time* have been pub-lished by Americans who have immigrated to San Miguel de Allen-de; these books are filled with rich descriptions of the "quaint" and "charming" city, a perfect place for an American to flee to, leaving the fast-paced world of commercialism and technology behind. This pleasant and whimsical opinion is shared by many Americans who live in San Miguel. I often met American expatriates in the Jardin, an open public garden in the center of the city. All the ex-pats I spoke to have sentiments that echo the sentiments of these novels, and their feelings on what makes San Miguel more desirable than America of-ten came up in conversation. I even met several retired persons who proudly proclaimed that they did not even need to learn any Spanish to live in San Miguel. One woman who had immigrated from Texas five years ago told me that she had only learned enough Spanish to communicate requests to her maids. Book clubs, yoga, social groups, and small church congregations created by *gringos* can be found throughout the city, forming small pockets of Americanness within the greater Mexican culture.

Meanwhile, the Mexican people of San Miguel have adapted to the influx of immigrants and tourists and utilized them as a source of income. For example, the city has three professional language schools, along with multiple hotels, day spas, and *gringo*-friendly book stores that carry popular novels in English exclusively. Two of my host sisters, aged 23 and 26, worked for a real estate company that primarily dealt with what they referred to as the "older rich white people who live on the hill." Indeed, many of the Americans live in large houses situated on the hillsides that look down into San Miguel proper.

This symbiotic relationship between the two cultures raises the question of identity for both groups of people. Certainly each ex-pat has his or her own reason for immigrating to San Miguel, but most do not seem to feel that it is necessary to assimilate completely into Mexican culture; hence, the self-imposed segregation and exclusive nature of the "pockets" of Americans in the city. These people have certainly retained the identity of what it is to be "American," although they claim that they want nothing more to do with America as a country. Several of the elderly people that I spoke to told me that the reason they left America was that the government was too horrible to stand anymore; however, they still desired certain creature comforts that they would find back in America, such as cell phone reception, Internet access, and TV shows like *Law and Order* and *CSI*. One woman, who attended the same language school as I did, fretted about how difficult it was to find her favorite foods in the city's small grocery stores. These things suggest that the American populations still retained their previous collective identity and collective memory.

However, the gringo population, despite its desire for certain personal creature comforts, seemed to be quite concerned with preserving San Miguel de Allende as a city, and they were obsessed with keeping it a charming historical (i.e., old-fashioned) and—most important—Mexican town. At least, what they perceived to be Mexican. For example, when a Subway and a Dunkin' Donuts opened in the town center and a McDonald's arrived just outside the city proper, it caused a great uproar in the gringo population. I asked ex-pats in the city how they felt about the fast food chains, and the response was almost unanimously negative. Only one gentleman I spoke to was pleased to have his morning coffee from Dunkin' Donuts. Many Americans had boycotted the restaurants, because the consensus was that it was "ruining the charm and authenticity of the city" and that the restaurants were not "Mexican enough." The thing that concerned the American townspeople the most was that these chain stores were ruining the Mexican history of the city with American culture.

That buzz-word "authenticity" was what sparked my curiosity on this subject. What did the ex-pat population perceive to be truly, authentically Mexican about the city, and what did they perceive to be spoiling the atmosphere? Certainly the appearance of American chain restaurants was a great disappointment for the gringos. Did the Mexican people feel that these chains were "not Mexican enough" as well? The response I received from Mexican people about these chains was either general complaints about how the food was too expensive, or comments like "it's just a restaurant, like any other." I learned from the Mexican family that I stayed with that being traditional was not the most important thing to them. Eating instant ramen noodles and pizza, watching *American Idol* after dinner, and wearing Nike shoes did not strike them as being problematic. The concept of the collective memory of what it is to be Mexican was seated much deeper than these sorts of superficial things. The time when Mexican identity really came to the forefront was on religious and secular holidays.

During my stay in San Miguel, I observed religious and secular celebrations, from the Mexican Independence Day to small local church celebrations of patron saints. A common element for each holiday that I observed was a large and complex parade that wended its way through the center of the city. These parades were similar in that each one pertained to the history of the city and of Mexico as a whole. Each parade included specific Works Cited to this history, including Aztec dancing, religious icons such as the Virgin of Guadalupe, impersonations of key figures in Mexican history, larger-than-life Frida Kahlo dolls, and reenactors depicting Mexican Revolution battle scenes.

Such celebrations raise the question of collective memory versus "authenticity" in this highly touristic city. In their paper "After Authenticity at an American Heritage Site," Gable and Handler (1996) raise the question of authentic reproduction in Colonial Williamsburg and conclude, among other things, that Americans are obsessed with historical accuracy. Can this be applied to San Miguel de Allende as well, an area so heavily influenced by a wealthy American population? Does the Mexican population of San Miguel direct their celebrations to the tourists and the ex-pats who wish to see the "real" history of Mexico? After all, San Miguel receives a great deal of revenue from tourists and foreign residents, and the Mexican residents of San Miguel recognize them as a healthy source of income. I often asked the Mexican people about their relationships with the tourist and ex-pat culture. I spoke to shopkeepers and owners of Internet cafes and the Mexican doorman at a hotel and day spa that was oriented mostly towards foreign visitors. Whenever I spoke to them about the American retired population and the tourists, they responded simply, "Ellos traen más dinero," "They bring in more money." The times in which the tourists and ex-pats really bring in the most money for the Mexican citizens of San Miguel is during the holidays and festivals, and so one has to wonder whether or not the Mexican residents strive to create an authentic performance to appease the tourists and bring in more money to the city. Are these celebrations reflections of how Mexican people of San Miguel view history, or are the parades and festivities featured in these holidays organized to cater to the tourist population?

In this paper, I analyze three of the parades that I observed during three separate holidays while I was living in San Miguel. The reason I have chosen parades as my window in which to see the Mexican idea of memory and identity is that a parade is a visual representation that involves the entire city, some as performers and some as spectators. Parades are used to act out events and create larger-than-life, enhanced representations of people and places without the need for speech. I also chose parades as my focus because I learned very quickly that in Mexico, it was practically unthinkable to hold any sort of festival or holiday without a parade, so it was easy to compare and contrast each celebration through this common element. These three parades that I have chosen to compare and contrast took place on El Dia de San Miguel (San Miguel Day), El Dia de Independencia (September 16th, the Mexican Independence Day), and the saint's day of a small local church. I chose these three parades because each one was distinctive in its purpose. El Dia de Independencia is a secular, historical celebration that celebrates the history of Mexican freedom and independence, a celebration of Mexico as a nation. Meanwhile, El Dia de San Miguel is a celebration that focuses on the Catholic Archangel Michael, who is also the patron saint of the city. The small saint's-day celebration that took place in one of the town's many Catholic churches is a representation of the religion of Mexican people at a local, more personal, family level.

El Dia de Independencia occurs throughout Mexico on September 16th, not just in the city of San Miguel; and thus it is truly a representation of national identity. The parade that occurred during this holiday was large and complex and included elements taken from throughout the history of Mexico. The most common element in the parade itself was a huge number of Aztec dancers. After almost every float, jazz or mariachi band, or group of horseback riders, there would be a troupe of Aztec dancers. One could tell that each group felt itself to be distinctive because they often carried a banner denoting what tribe they traced their ancestry to. Furthermore, each group had a very specific costume, complete with plumed headdresses and skulls. I concluded that this representation of Aztec dancing represents the very heart of Mexican identity.

Florescano (1994) explains that the Aztecs still represent the oldest and one of the most important aspects of Mexican history, and to be involved in such a reenactment is a preeminent honor. Judging by the sheer number of Aztec dancers involved in the parade for El Dia De Independencia, this is certainly a true statement. However, as important as authentic-appearing reenactment may be, I noticed that many of the dancers wore normal everyday sneakers and carried water bottles. I even saw one particular dancer wearing what looked like a pair of pajama bottoms rather than the same garb as his fellows. I asked my host sister why it was not "accurate," and she laughed and told me, "It is all just for fun, we don't know exactly how the Aztecs danced."

Another element, almost as popular as the Aztec reenactors, was the reenactors of historical Mexico. Members of the parade dressed as heroes of the Revolution—e.g., Allende and Hidalgo—marched down the streets, mock-fighting French, Spanish, and indigenous soldiers alike; while Pancho Villas, flamenco dancers, and papier-mâché Frida mannequins cavorted along behind them. At first this too did not make sense to me, because the time sequence appeared to be off. The battles that the parade was re-creating did not flow in any sort of time that I could see. However, I have concluded that this seemingly haphazard sequence of events is in fact the way that the Mexican mind views time and memory. As Florescano states, "Thus, if for western thought an event is historical only, it is produced in a profane time and space, stripped of transcendental meaning. For the Mexica mentality, the historical is exactly the opposite: the event that has weight is the one that is endowed with significance that transcends the time and place in which it is located." Therefore, the Mexican mentality is that the correct way in which to pay one's respect to the past is not through fiercely accurate representation, but through the simple act of remembering the significant aspects of the events. Many gringos attended this celebration, but when I asked in the next week at my language school what everyone's thoughts were on the parade, not a single person broached the subject of the authenticity of the performance. Before the celebration began, I spoke to one American who spends his summers in San Miguel, and he mentioned that El Dia de Independencia was the only San Miguel holiday that he and his wife attended every year. This is obviously a popular holiday among gringos, and yet they did not seem to be concerned with the nonlinear time that the parade had illustrated.

The second parade that I attended occurred on El Dia de San Miguel. El Dia de San Miguel is a week-long celebration during the last week of September. This holiday recognizes the town's patron saint, the archangel Michael. It is a religious time for the community, but also a time for frivolity. During the course of the week of celebrations, there are several parades, which become bigger and more elaborate as the week goes on. On San Miguel day itself, the most important part of the celebration occurs at around midnight. This event is the biggest parade of the week, followed by an hour-long firework display outside the city's largest church at around midnight. I was told by my host family that this sequence of events represents St. Michael's descent into the Underworld to battle Lucifer. The parade itself, which lasted a good thirty to forty-five minutes, included the usual elements: troupes of Aztec dancers accompanied only by drumbeat, and mariachi and jazz bands whose music clashed spectacularly with the Aztec drumbeats. However, the two defining qualities of this parade were crosses and religious icons made out of colored paper with candles placed in the middle and carried over the crowd, along with elaborately constructed bundles of flowers that were placed all around the Parroquia and given out to members of the crowd. A young woman walked in the middle of the parade dressed as the Archangel Michael, followed by other women and girls also dressed as angels. Priests and religious officials followed the women, singing and bearing incense and banners depicting the virgin of Guadalupe, blessing members of the crowd as they walked. This parade was unique because it was purely for religious purposes rather than to depict historical events. This does not make the events any less real for the Mexican people, however. The revolutionary heroes depicted in the Independence Day parade are as much a mythic reality as the Archangel Michael. According to Leenhardt (1979), "myth and person are so closely interwoven that we see them support each other, proceed from each other, stabilize each other...and justify each other." Leenhardt was writing about Melanesians, but what he says is equally true of the attitude of the Mexicans of San Miguel to holy figures and historical heroes.

The two celebrations that I have described so far are instances in which the presence of tourists and non-Mexican members of the community is not only expected, but encouraged. Both El Dia de San Miguel and el Dia de Independencia are very important when it comes to the economy of the city. But the evidence of these rituals strongly suggests that American influence on the city does not extend to the way that the Mexicans present their history and memory through parade and celebration. The Mexican concept of authenticity and identity differs strikingly from the American concept, even in a melting-pot city such as San Miguel, where culture is exchanged every day. This conclusion was confirmed again for me later in my stay, when it was possible for me to observe a parade that was intended for a smaller and more private audience. In this case, the audience was a small local church that my host family belonged to.

This celebratory parade was in honor of the patron saint of my host-family church. It was a very small parade in an area outside the town center. Because of this setting, my roommate and I were the only two gringas present. This parade turned out to be a small version of the parade I witnessed on San Miguel day. There were a small group of Aztec dancers, religious officials bearing crosses and incense, and community members bearing bundles of flowers that they placed upon altars in the streets until the parade reached its destination, the local church, just in time for mass.

What interested me most about this smaller parade is that it was not meant to cater to a tourist community. Therefore, the members of the parade were not showing off or acting in any way. This was a celebration that reflected only the religious ideas of a local community, and yet it was performed in the same way that the large public parades were carried out. This leads me to the conclusion that although San Miguel hopes to draw in the wealth of the tourist and ex-pat populations, their traditions in celebration remain Mexican, almost entirely unaffected by the ex-pat presence.

I went to Mexico with the intent to learn Spanish and take a vacation, but I could not help analyzing the vivid culture of the city San Miguel de Allende. Through this research, I had hoped to learn more about the collective identity and memory of the two most prominent groups that live in the city, the Mexicans and the gringos. I also hoped to paint a realistic picture of how the Mexican people of San Miguel view and identify with the past as a collective. Despite the considerable migration and cultural exchange between Mexican and gringo populations, the Mexican residents do not attempt to re-create the past in such a way that is pleasing for the tourist and expatriate cultures. The Mexican people have a very different concept of what is authentic. Rather, the goal of these celebrations is to honor and remember key points in the past. Of course, two months spent in any location is not enough, and I hope to return to Mexico this summer before I begin pursuing graduate studies. While there I hope to gather more information on this topic and continue my research.

WORKS CITED

Christenson, Allen J. 2001. *Art and Society in a Highland Maya Community*. Austin: University of Texas Press.

Cohan, Tony. 2000. *On Mexican Time: A New Life in San Miguel*. New York: Broadway Books.

Florescano, Enrique. 1994. *Memory, Myth, and Time in Mexico: From the Aztecs to Independence*. Austin: University of Texas Press.

Gable, Eric, and Richard Handler. 1996. "After Authenticity at an American Heritage Site." *American Anthropologist* 98(3):568-578.

Halbwachs, Maurice. 1992. *On Collective Memory*. Chicago: University of Chicago Press.

Leenhardt, Maurice. 1979. *Do Kamo: Person and Myth in the Melanesian World*. Chicago: University of Chicago Press.

Sahlins, Marshall. 1981. *Historical Metaphors and Mythical Realities*. Ann Abor: University of Michigan Press.

Schmidt, Carol, and Norma Hair. 2006. *Falling...in Love with San Miguel: Retiring to Mexico on Social Security*. Laredo, TX: Salsa Verde Press.

Moving around in the Room: Cherokee Language, Worldview and Memory

Heidi M. Altman, Georgia Southern University
Thomas N. Belt, Cherokee, Western Carolina University

For the past year we have been examining aspects of Cherokee language and worldview as they relate to health and native understandings of well-being. As a part of this work we have previously described the system of well-being encoded in Cherokee language and how Cherokee speakers view the processes of history (Altman and Belt 2009, Altman and Belt 2008). In brief, Cherokee speakers view the proper state of the world as being *tohi*, or operating according to the processes and pace of nature. In addition, the proper state of individual people in the world is *osi*, which is conceptualized as upright, forward-facing, and existing on a single point of balance. In order for the world to be in its proper state, individuals must also be properly balanced. Much of Cherokee traditional medicine, healing, and wellness is centered around processes designed to return people and the world to these interrelated states. These ideas extend beyond the personal, however. Cherokee views of history also try to understand past events within this framework and then try to determine the proper course for the future.

Prompting our work on these issues has been a practical concern that stems from our work with the Culturally Based Native Health Programs, a suite of community-initiated cultural competency initiatives directed by our colleague Lisa Lefler, Ph.D., with the Eastern Band of Cherokee Indians. We are developing a basis for educating

health-care providers to a better understanding of traditional practices, both for elders who are still Cherokee speakers and for younger
generations who have been reared with traditional Cherokee values
regarding health and well-being.

As a part of studying health and well-being in Indian communities, the issue of multigenerational grief and trauma, or intergenera-
tional trauma, is a constant presence—sometimes in the foreground,
sometimes in the background. The past 15-20 generations, since
Cherokee people came into extensive contact with Europeans, have
been faced with widespread traumatic events that repeatedly turned
their world upside down. Disease, population loss, economic depen-
dence, loss of crucial aspects of medicine, persistent European wars
and skirmishes, rape, the burning of towns, murder, violence, the
Removal, the Civil War, economic disenfranchisement, the boarding
school experience, and on and on—all these events and processes
forced the Cherokees to adapt continually to new and deleterious
circumstances. In reviewing this history we began to discuss the lan-
guage-based cognitive structures speakers use in processing memory, the past, and experiences that are significant but not necessarily
immediately at hand. As these discussions progressed, we realized
that these cognitive processes must be taken into consideration in
developing programs to address multigenerational grief and trauma
in Cherokee communities, and that their analogues in other communities might be instructive as well.

CHEROKEE LANGUAGE

The Cherokee language is an Iroquoian language, distantly related
to the languages of the Six Nations of New York and Canada. Classi-
fied as a polysynthetic language, Cherokee and the other Iroquoian
languages have extremely complex inflectional morphology that

provides speakers with the ability to convey very specific and nu-
anced meaning in the conjugation of verbs alone. In addition, Cherokee is marvelously complex in its inclusion of tone or stress distinctions or both, morphophonemic complexity that often obscures
roots of verbs, and the simple extent of its class of pronominal pre-
fixes (60+ possibilities), among other features.

Part of the verbal morphology of Cherokee is an aspect system
that marks the quality of actions in verbs, and that in many ways
takes the place of the tense system that English speakers rely on. In
English, events described by verbs are obligatorily tied to a linear
timeline that indicates past, present, or future. English also uses, to
a lesser extent, some grammatical indicators of aspect—to demonstrate that an action is ongoing or completed, for example; however
many of these kinds of distinctions are made lexically rather than
grammatically in English. In Cherokee, however, a speaker can use
a variety of aspects to describe the quality of the action (e.g., ongoing, punctative, completed, habitual, reported) without necessarily
tying the action to any particular point in time. Tense can be used by
speakers if desired; it is not obligatory, however. As a result, Cherokee speakers can easily tell stories about events that happened in the
past with an immediacy not grammatically possible in English—or
at least not through simply conjugating a verb.

METAPHORS FOR TIME AND SPACE

Given the grammar of English, English speakers tend to conceptualize and construct spatial metaphors for time as a linear, forward-
flowing process. In any given utterance in English, one can place
the action at some point along a timeline. Our metaphors describe
this concept with common phrases like "you've got your whole fu-
ture <u>ahead</u> of you" or "the past is all <u>behind</u> you now." Also, at least

since the industrial age, we have specified this metaphor further by quantifying ever-smaller units of time, now even down to the nano-second. In this way, the further along the timeline an event is from the speaker's present moment, the greater the conceptual distance between the speaker and the event. Thus in describing or discussing the events of the past, English speakers have a built-in sense of dis-tance in space, as well as of duration.

Cherokee speakers, on the other hand, do not have a linear con-cept for time and space. The grammar of Cherokee permits a meta-phor for the process of time and distance that is infinitely flexible. Rather than seeing events as beads on a string or points on a line that must always occur in the same order with the same distance between them, Cherokee speakers conceive of time (or life) as a room one enters by one door at birth and leaves by another at death. All of the possible events that have happened, are happening, or will hap-pen exist in this room. Over the course of one's life one may interact with the various events that have transpired, or those that have yet to do so, in various ways. We have discussed the process of reading the past elsewhere (Altman and Belt 2008); in short, Cherokee speak-ers have the conceptual ability to move about in the room and pick up and examine events at any point they wish. So when a Cherokee speaker talks about the Removal, she or he can do so with a sense that the events of that time are still here with us, immediate and ongoing.

THE LANGUAGE OF MEMORY

Supporting the metaphors for memory and time, Cherokee speakers have linguistically-encoded models for where memory resides in the body and how it moves from place to place within the body over time. As time passes, the location and fixedness of memories change. For Cherokee speakers, memory has two parts or processes (short-term and long-term memory) and these are associated with different parts of the body (the head and the heart). For Cherokee speakers, short-term memories reside in the head. When someone has experienced something recently, they can refer to those experiences using simple sense-based phrases such as *tsigoha* ("I saw it") or *gigvha* ("I heard it"). These verbs are minimally conjugated to include only the person marker, the stem of the verb, and the *–ha* suffix that indicates that the act is complete. As people refer to events in this form, the events themselves are open to interpretation by the individual and his or her interlocutors. If a person wonders about the significance of an event, he or she can discuss it with others to arrive at an appropriate understanding of why the event happened and what it can tell them. In sum, memories of recent events are sense-based, reside in the head, are flexible in their interpretation and open to social construction. Of course, not every event that happens to an individual undergoes this process of analysis and verification, but all are open to it if the speaker feels it necessary.

After about a month, memories that have been interpreted and verified, or that did not need to be interpreted or verified, pass from the head to the heart. For Cherokee speakers, memory, as properly understood separate from events that are still flexible, resides in the heart as an accumulated deposit of indelible experiences. Once memory moves to the heart, not only is it indelible, but it is referred to with different words. These words include *ahndisdi* ("memory"), *gadahntehv* ("I am remembering" or "I am thinking"), *agwadahnta* ("my heart feels") a particular way, and *nohsahna* ("out of sorts"). Each of these words in Cherokee has, at its root, the morpheme *–ahn*, which refers to the heart. Terms that refer to heart/feeling/memory are often used in determining how to treat a patient in the traditional system. The connection between events, memory, and beliefs about health is reflected in this aspect of the traditional Cherokee worldview. For Cherokee practitioners there are states of being ill that relate to feelings in addition to those that are specifically disease- or injury-related. Understanding the relationships between the heart/feeling/memory terms and health and wellness is the focus of the next stage of our work on this system.

In addition to the words and metaphors for remembering and memory, Cherokee has metaphorical language for forgetting. As mentioned above, we have described elsewhere the Cherokee system for examining or reading the past (Altman and Belt 2008), in which one can move around in the metaphorical room of life and pick up events as one chooses. The language for forgetting is related to this process conceptually. To say "I am forgetting," a Cherokee speaker says *agikewsga*. This verb shares its root with the word *dikewi* or "blind." So for a Cherokee speaker, forgetting is literally not being able to see something that has happened in the past. Events become forgotten to a speaker because his or her heart/mind cannot see them in the big room of life. In some instances, speakers cannot see because they are being protected by their heart/mind from something that has happened. Sometimes events cannot be seen for simpler reasons that are more akin to the English-speaker's concept of forgetting. In either case, when a Cherokee speaker has forgotten something, he or she is unable to "examine or read" the past event or object in the sense we outlined above, or *agoliye*.

SIGNIFICANCE FOR APPLICATION AND CONCLUSIONS

Our examination of memory and language among Cherokee speakers has significance in terms of its application in both direct health care and health-care education settings. In the health-care setting, understanding Cherokee concepts of the process of memory and

forgetting allows health-care providers new perspectives on the con-
stellation of behavioral and medical health issues lumped together
under the name multigenerational grief and trauma. Insights into
the immediacy that Cherokee speakers feel about past traumatic
events, and the cultural values passed on by Cherokee speakers to
their non-Cherokee-speaking family members, allow providers to
realize that there are culturally-grounded methods for dealing with
seeing and not seeing what is in the room. These methods, encoded
in language and embodied in traditions, are largely missing from
existing treatment models.

In the health-care education setting, we advocate that practitioners be educated as to the variety of different ways that speakers of
any language other than English may conceptualize their understanding of the world. The bridge between cultures must be built on
understandings that become available only by developing herme-
neutic models based in language.

WORKS CITED

Altman, Heidi, and Thomas N. Belt. 2008. "Reading History:
Cherokee History Through a Cherokee Lens." *Native South*
1:90-98.

_____. 2009. "Tohi: The Cherokee State of Well-Being." In *Under
the Rattlesnake: Cherokee Health and Resiliency*, edited by
Lisa Lefler, 9-22. Tuscaloosa: University of Alabama Press.

Contributors

HEIDI M. ALTMAN is Associate Professor of Anthropology at Georgia Southern University. Her specialties include linguistic anthropology, language revitalization and language, and health and worldview.

THOMAS N. BELT is Community Language Coordinator at the Cherokee Language Program, Western Carolina University.

BOBBY R. BRALY is a Research Assistant and doctoral candidate at the Frank H. McClung Museum, Department of Anthropology, at the University of Tennessee. He is most recently the author, with Shannon R. Koerner and Lynne P. Sullivan, of "A Reassessment of the Chronology of Mound A at Toqua," *Southeastern Archaeology* 30(1), 134-147.

AVI BRISMAN is an adjunct assistant professor at the John Jay College of Criminal Justice, the City University of New York (CUNY), where he teaches criminology and urban sociology. He is also a Ph.D. candidate in the Department of Anthropology at Emory University, where is writing his dissertation on legal consciousness.

JENNIFER CLINTON is the zooarchaeology lab coordinator and an adjunct faculty member in the Department of Sociology and Anthropology at Middle Tennessee State University. Her research interests focus geographically on the southeastern United States and thematically on general foodways studies, specifically the maintenance of animal related subsistence activities.

JOHN M. COGGESHALL is a Professor of Anthropology in the Department of Sociology and Anthropology at Clemson University, South Carolina. As a cultural anthropologist he is interested in the ways in which people become embedded into landscapes through stories, ownership, occupation, place names, and burials, thus forging a deeply emotional tie to the land. His research focuses on South Carolina's Blue Ridge area.

ERIC GABLE teaches cultural anthropology at the University of Mary Washington. He is the author, with Richard Handler, of *The New History in an Old Museum: Creating the Past at Colonial Williamsburg* (Duke University Press, 1997) and of *Anthropology and Egalitarianism: Ethnographic Encounters from Monticello to Guinea-Bissau* (Indiana University Press, 2011). He is currently a managing editor for *Museum and Society* and book reviews editor for *American Ethnologist*.

LAURA GALKE is an archaeologist for The George Washington Foundation. Her research is contributing to a richer understanding of George Washington's childhood and the role that historical narratives serve in contemporary society. Her published works include analyses of the material culture of 19th-century African American spirituality, of 17th-century European and American Indian contact in the Chesapeake, antebellum college surveillance strategies on the campus of Washington and Lee University, and the mid-18th-century consumer strategies of George Washington's mother.

RICHARD HANDLER is Dean of the Undergraduate College of Arts and Sciences, Professor of Anthropology, and Director of the Program in Global Development Studies at the University of Virginia.

He is a cultural anthropologist who studies modern western societies, with particular interest in nationalism, ethnicity, and the politics of culture. His publications include *Critics Against Culture: Anthropological Observers of Mass Society* (University of Wisconsin Press, 2005); *The New History in an Old Museum: Creating the Past at Colonial Williamsburg*, with Eric Gable (Duke University Press, 1997); and *Nationalism and the Politics of Culture in Quebec* (University of Wisconsin Press, 1988).

MARGARET WILLIAMSON HUBER is Distinguished Professor Emerita at the University of Mary Washington in Fredericksburg, Virginia. Her primary research interests are Native North America, especially the Southeast; Oceania, especially Melanesia; American popular culture; gender; and symbolic systems. Her book, *Powhatan Lords of Life and Death*, was published in 2003 by the University of Nebraska Press.

SHANNON KOERNER is an archaeologist at the Center for Environmental Management of Military Lands at Colorado State University. Her specialties include the prehistoric archaeology of the Southeast. She is the author, most recently, of "A Reassessment of the Chronology of Mound A at Toqua," with Bobby R. Braly and Lynne P. Sullivan, *Southeastern Archaeology* 30(1), 134-147.

SAM KRAUSE is a GIS analyst and archaeology field technician for Four Corners Research in Tularosa, New Mexico, and GIS analyst and excavation crew chief for the Maya Research Program. She specializes in mapping and survey.

BERNARD K. MEANS is an instructor in anthropology at the School of World Studies at Virginia Commonwealth University, Richmond, Virginia, and Director of the Virtual Curation Archaeology. His scholarly pursuits include reconstructing American Indian village

life from cross-cultural studies of village spatial and social organizations, the research potential of archaeological collections, and the
history of New Deal archaeology across America.

VINCENT MELOMO of William Peace University in Raleigh, North
Carolina, is an anthropologist who wears several hats. His primary
research and teaching interests are in the ethnic diversity of the U.S.,
with a specific focus on South Asian American youth. However, he
also has conducted research in historical archaeology. His contribution to this volume, "The Jamestown Commemoration of 2007:
Remembering our Diversity in the Past and Present," marries both
these interests.

JENNIFER WILLIAMS NOURSE is Associate Professor of Anthropology and Women, Gender and Sexuality Studies at University of Richmond. Her book, *Conceiving Spirits: Birth Rituals and Contested
Identities among Lauje of Indonesia*, was published by Smithsonian
Press in 1999. She recently completed a Fulbright project on medical
anthropology in Indonesia, and she is working on a new book on
perceptions of biomedicine in Muslim Indonesia.

TANYA M. PERES is Associate Professor of Anthropology at Middle
Tennessee State University. Her research interests are concerned
with the relationships between humans and their environments and
how these relationships impacted both the humans and other organ-
isms around them in a variety of times and places. She has published
widely in such journals as *Historical Archaeology, Tennessee Archaeology*, and *Current Research in the Pleistocene*; and she is co-editor,
with Amber VanDerwarker, of *Integrating Zooarchaeology and
Paleoethnobotany* (Springer Press, 2010).

SUSAN ELIZABETH PROBASCO is a doctoral candidate at the
University of Arkansas, where she holds a Walton Foundation

Doctoral Academy Fellowship. In 2011 Probasco returned to her alma mater, Clemson University, as a visiting lecturer in Anthropology. Research interests include southern culture, community attachment/topophilia, sacralization of space, oral history, and regional identities. Probasco's dissertation centering on two communities in the northernmost and southernmost counties of the Arkansas Delta is forthcoming.

LYNNE P. SULLIVAN is Curator of Archaeology at the Frank H. McClung Museum and Adjunct Professor of Anthropology at the University of Tennessee, Knoxville. Her specialties include the prehistoric archaeology of the Southeast and museology. Recent publications include *Mississippian Mortuary Practices: Beyond Hierarchy and the Representationalist Perspective*, edited with Robert C. Mainfort, Jr., Florida Museum of Natural History, Ripley P. Bullen Series (University Press of Florida, Gainesville, 2010); and *Curating Archaeological Collections: From the Field to the Repository*, with S. Terry Childs (Alta Mira Press, 2003).

www.ingramcontent.com/pod-product-compliance
Lightning Source LLC
Chambersburg PA
CBHW030303290526
45785CB00001B/195